EAST END MY CRADLE

WILLY GOLDMAN

East End My Cradle

Portrait of an Environment

faber and faber

This edition first published in 2011
by Faber and Faber Ltd
Bloomsbury House, 74–77 Great Russell Street
London WC1B 3DA

A CIP record for this book is available from the British Library

ISBN 978–0–571–27646–2

In loving memory of my sister,
Lillian Hilliard (1903–1984)
of Ventura, California, USA

and of

Professor Frieda Goldman-Eisler
(1907–1982), Founder and Director of
the Psycholinguistics Department
of the University of London

and with

gratitude to John Lehmann (1907–1987),
author and editor of *New Writing*
and *The London Magazine*,
for help and encouragement

I have no song of praise
No words of love
For cats or gods or daffodils,
But I have tried to leave
For ever in your mind
The noise that men make
When they break their chains.
                        Paul Potts,
                        Poet's Testament

Contents

7

PART III

PART IV

Introduction

IN my compulsive forays into London's East End—until recently a secret pilgrimage—I now take my wife along. Although the sensations evoked during these travels cannot, strictly, be shared, she being no East-Ender, there is a certain absurd element in it that we can, because of its appeal to both our natures, share: when in the course of our perambulations I bring us to a sudden halt at some street the look in her eye says: 'Don't tell me—another memory!'

Yes, another bloody memory, in both senses of that epithet: the literal and the nostalgic. Why should one be nostalgic about memories that are bloody? Is it related to that even bloodier memory that often impels survivors from a battlefield on a similar periodical pilgrimage in the attempt to make contact with a former intenser, more vivid, self? The denizen of a slum *is* like a soldier in battle. He is fighting for his very life. No stakes could be higher. He lives always amidst the cries of the fallen and wherever he goes he cannot avoid the sight of the walking wounded. He is aware constantly that his own time could be at hand. Survival itself is a victory.

Looking back later it is not the horror but the tenacity with which he fought it that he cherishes. Returning to the scene enhances the miracle of his survival. Nor can he forgo wallowing in some degree in a kind of regret for the loss of feeling that his triumph over adversity must inevitably entail. He has lived at a pitch he cannot help but value (like the Biblical price of a Virtuous Woman) as beyond rubies.

At any rate, it's the way I see it. There are surviving landmarks in my Stepney but it's the gaps that tug at the heart:

Hessel Street market at the top of our turning, called

'Morgan Street' by the older generation, that being the name it bore when they arrived here in the late nineteenth century. To us children it was a happy hunting ground for dislodged fruit rotting beneath the kerbside barrows.

The Johnny Walker distillery in Commercial Road whose powerful early-morning hooter summoning its employees to work reached the most distant home, prompting the reflection: Send not to know for whom the hooter hoots . . .

Directly across the road is Gowers Walk, a narrow, cobbled, dingy byway inhabited solely by factories and warehouses where at night in its crannies and doorways the shilling-a-time prostitutes plied their grisly trade.

Glamorous nights 'up the People's': the People's Palace in the Mile End Road, Mecca for the Saturday-night dance for those in work who could pay the shilling-and-sixpence admission. Those young patrons who had failed to lure a dance partner for the stroll home afterwards wended their sad way to Vallance Road to appease their sorrow at the fish shop on the corner with two-penn'orth of chips. The enterprising householder next door had rigged up in his front-room window a metal draining-board and tap from which he dispensed thrupenny glasses of fizzy lemonade to the thirsty gobblers of hot chips.

The Mission for the Conversion of the Jews to Christianity to which we ambled after signing on at the Labour Exchange on Mondays. Good for a free bun-and-tea if you put on a pious face and joined in the singing of evangelical hymns. My mother had occasionally taken me there in infancy for the free medical treatment doled out for minor ailments. As she did not understand a word of the sermon or singing she was no doubt able to persuade herself that she was not being tainted by association with apostasy. The Meeting always began with:

> *I'm snuggling close to Jesus*
> *Closer every day . . .*

Our favourite chant went,

> *There ain't no flies on Jesus,*
> *There ain't no flies on Christ,*
> *There may be flies on you and me,*
> *But there ain't no flies on dear J.C.*

Halfway through, an old man at the back of the Hall sprang to his feet and yelled: 'I'll kill the bleed'n lot o' yer!' He did this every week and it's what we'd come for, as well as to see him pitched out by the attendants; the bun-and-tea a mere bonus. We thought it odd that they always let him in the following week. Did they hope to reform him?

The political meetings: held in the open air and attended by large crowds and incessant heckling. Vallance Road—immortalised since as the gangster HQ of the Kray brothers—was a popular venue. So was Canon Street Road at the Commercial Road end. There in the 1931 General Election I witnessed the memorable debate between Liberal candidate Barnett Janner and Communist Harry Pollitt, both masters of political rhetoric. There, too: Oswald Mosley's 'New Party'—his choice of Parliamentary candidate a Jew: Ted 'Kid' Lewis, former World Welterweight Boxing Champion, 'idol of the East End', squanderer of a fortune from the Ring, down on his uppers and grist to Mosley's mill.

The Workers' Circle in Great Alie Street, a building co-operatively owned and administered by the various Socialist sections in the locality where, among its nightly functions, radical plays and lectures were a notable feature. One I attended had as guest speaker the redoubtable international radical, Emma Goldman (dubbed 'Red Emma' by the world's press). She had been a leader of the Social Revolutionary Party during and following the 1917 Russian Revolution and quarrelled with Lenin over his dictatorial policies before retreating into exile in the USA. At our meeting she was subjected to orchestrated barracking and heckling by the Communist faction in the audience, but she gave as good as she got.

I had for some time been stirred into an awakening political consciousness, but as a topic it was unrewarding at home. My mother's less-than-panoramic view had remained stuck in World War I when, as we cowered in the cellar during the German air raids, her reiterated curse upon our then Prime Minister could be heard above the exploding bombs: 'A fire on Lloyd George!'

My father, also simplistic in his views and indeed repelled by anything requiring mental exertion, was a supporter of Authority, currently invested in Prime Minister Stanley Baldwin to whom he was particularly partial, perhaps for the flattering reason that the latter's inertia on the public front matched his own on the domestic one. When I voiced criticism he retorted, 'So you know better dan Mister Baldvin? So tell me, please—fer vy don' dey make *you* der Prime Minister?'

I was not what Jewish parents called 'a good son'. I refused to converse with them in Yiddish, they had to muster what English they could when desiring verbal communication. Following my barmitzvah at the age of thirteen I ceased accompanying my grandfather to the synagogue in Brick Lane on the Sabbath and was castigated by him as 'a Yiddisher Goy!'

He was widowed in 1918 and had since lived the life of a recluse, turning a bleak, unseeing face to the world. He occupied our single ground-floor front room. There he kept his stock of cutlery and women's hosiery in large crates which, daily, not long after dawn, he loaded on to his barrow outside in the gutter and pushed it the mile-long journey to Petticoat Lane where he had a stall and pushed it all the way back at the day's end to unload again in his front room. It must have reminded him of life in *der Heim* in Russia where the goats and chickens shared the living space. His room smelled as if they still did.

His sole recreations were studying the learned commen-
taries of the Hebrew *Rashi* and kicking the cat, the latter an
activity with diminishing returns, since in the course of time
the cat learned to identify the sound of my grandfather's
footsteps descending the stairs on his way to our cellar
living-room and would abdicate its niche by the fire and
attempt a stealthy exit before he arrived. He despised it for
its indolence. He believed that everyone should work — not a
popular tenet in our family — and saw no reason for the
four-legged community to be exempt from this draconian
creed.

He himself went to bed at nine p.m. and rose at five a.m.
for an hour's devotion to prayer, ritually berobed in skull-
cap, *tallus* and *twillin*, before setting off to Petticoat Lane for
the day's toil. We children looked upon him as humourless;
but then he didn't have a lot to laugh about.

The old adage of someone being singled out as the 'black
sheep' of the family was reversed in many a home: it was the
'white sheep' who stood out, the sort who communicated
with his elders in Yiddish, accompanied his father to the
synagogue on the Sabbath, pursued a career in the sweat-
shop uncomplainingly, spent a good deal of his leisure at the
domestic hearth or 'going steady' with a young woman of
equally sober inclinations whom he would bring home to
meet his family and not frolic about with in dark alleyways of
an evening. I had in fact been for some time of the opinion
that all clerics of whatever faith were fraudulent, and
especially the sort togged up from top to toe in black hat,
black beard, long black overcoat, and ringlets dangling
down each ear. Whenever I encounter one of these frock-
coated apparitions with a wife in tow, I stop and stare and
reflect, 'Funny lot, women!' I now 'came out', as the saying
goes today for a different type of dissident, the homosexual.

My parents were never reconciled to my failure to gain
upwardly mobile status as a sweatshop worker ultimately
'making it' as a sweatshop proprietor. Years later at a family

chitchat round the table, after I had long been established as a toiler in the vineyards of Literature, my father confessed, casually, that he had always assumed (and still did, I gathered) that I earned my keep as a professional pimp. 'Vell, vot else is dere?' he reasoned. 'You don' gamble, you don' back horses, you von't vork at a proper trade—so vot's left?' To protest that authorship was 'a proper trade' sounded even to me somewhat feeble, so I said nothing. He warmed to his theme: 'You gotta be careful. It's a crime in England. You could finish up in de electric chair!'

Gone are those reeking tenements where the fleas outnumbered the residents. Tower blocks have replaced many of the cramped little houses on the narrow pavements, huddled together as if for warmth. Cellar-gratings were a conspicuous feature. With a long piece of string threaded through a hole in a cocoa-tin lid smeared with glue and let down by way of the grating one might pick up a dropped coin lost below. An equally popular gambit, when parents were absent, was to let yourselves through the downstairs living-room that opened on to the cellar and wait for a group of women to pause on the grating for a gossip so that you could look up their skirts.

The demolished White Chapel that gave its name to the area is now a patch of grass; former synagogues in Brick Lane are mosques; through the windows of the sweatshops that function the faces are Asian. Gone is Gardiners Corner, legendary meeting-place for lovers, for Sunday ramblers assembling for a day in the country, and the historic rallying site for the rout, in 1936, by the local citizenry of Oswald Mosley's intended fascist March through the East End.

In the dockside, a couple of streets distant from where our family lived, the local anthem boasted the title, 'No Jews Allowed Down Wapping'. Well, our kind have long departed. Now they've got Rupert Murdoch. Verily, God is not mocked.

Nevertheless, it is not a scene of desolation that I find

myself lamenting in the Keatsian sense that 'The sedge has withered from the lake/And no birds sing'. For me it is a scene where, like the warrior in war, my emotions were at their rawest; one of those whom Dostoievsky called 'the insulted and injured'. I treasure the memories while abhorring the social conditions that begat them. I am for ever a prisoner in this not too tender trap. I can never escape from it and I would never want to.

Willy Goldman
October 1987

PART ONE

CHAPTER I

Yids versus Goys

ANTI-SEMITISM, in my infancy, had its compensations, for being confined practically to children (I speak of anti-Semitism not as a subjective attitude but in its positive sense, as demonstrated in Germany), it never amounted to anything more serious than a kind of game. It was largely a pretext for staging occasional 'battles' between the Jews and Gentiles. Each party of children took up its stand and pelted the other across the no-man's-land of our narrow, cobbled street. For ammunition we used the rubbish from the dustbins and gutters. The 'battle' ended when the rubbish gave out; there was no ill will afterwards.

It is only since getting into adult hands that positive anti-Semitism in England has deteriorated from a sport into a tyranny.

I won't say that anti-Semitism was even then without its serious aspects. People living in the predominantly Jewish side of Stepney (Whitechapel) hardly dared venture into the predominantly Gentile side, Wapping. Abuse was the very least one could expect; a beer bottle across the head was the more likely penalty. True, it has to be admitted that the Gentiles didn't invade us. That is something we may reasonably expect if and when English politics sink to the level of those in pre-1939 Germany.

Our street had its own peculiar racial problem. Welk Street, as it is called, is part of that area between Wapping and Whitechapel known as St. Georges, a neighbourhood that is a kind of frontier to either, and in which therefore the populations show signs of the merging. Our street was a typical example. The Gentiles lived clustered together up one half, we occupied the other. You could tell which were which by the kind of cooking smells that greeted you when you passed a door. Our respective smells were quite different.

There was an unspoken hostility between us, but no actual displays of violence — except when the Gentiles returned home drunk from the pub at the corner. They would career noisily up the street, hurl abuse at the Jewish houses and occasionally send one of their 'empties' through a Jewish window. We sat silent and watchful behind our doors. It was a reminder to us that pogroms had not died with the Russian Tsar. We were contemptuous rather than afraid: we knew the Gentiles couldn't do very much to us in a free country like England. We waited patiently for the storm to pass. 'They don't know any better,' my mother explained sadly. 'They're only Goyim.'

We children took it less philosophically. We hadn't the memory of Tsarist pogroms to help us appreciate the comparative harmlessness of the current attacks. We felt ourselves English and outraged. We wanted to go and fling bottles at *their* windows. Our parents, when they got wind of such an idea, were shocked, and threatened to flay us alive. You couldn't argue with them. 'It's the Gentile's country,' my mother explained. 'He can do what he likes. In your country *you* will be master. You must have patience until the Messiah comes.' It seemed to us throwing away a very good opportunity for what was at best an 'outside' chance.

In the intervals between such incidents the Jewish and Gentile children bore each other no grudge. There were, of course, individual bullies here and there who ambushed a younger Jew, twisted his arm behind his back, and cried: 'Say that Christians are better'n Jews! Gorn, say it!'— and went on twisting until he did. These bullies were disapproved of by Jew and Gentile alike. For most of us 'anti-Semitism' was a kind of game or romantic feud. Our two groups mixed quite freely in the street games: Archie Griggs, for instance, was our centre-forward when we matched other street teams at football — even though he took opposite sides of the barricades in a 'battle'.

Differences between us (apart from physical ones) did exist. We, for instance, respected authority more than they. The Gentiles were contemptuous of it. If a policeman suddenly appeared at one of our street football games they would stand their ground and try to have it out with him:

'Gertch, y' mucking copper, you!'

They abused him from the opposite pavement, trying to provoke him into undignified chase. We would stand at a safe distance, shocked, but admiring.

Thinking it over now, I do not believe we were less brave than they. The street battles proved that. Also individual examples of courage: my elder brother comes to mind. I remember us both attending a Gentile school for three months during the Great War while living with a relative in another part of London. We were the only Jews. At lesson time we had to part, for I was six, and he was in the section of twelve-year-old boys. He waited for me at play-time in case of trouble. As expected, something like seventy-five per cent of the boys bore down upon us. They didn't know that my brother was one of the terrors of our neighbourhood. He didn't wait for the Gentiles to start things. He merely handed me his jacket and waded into the lot of them like a mad bull. He bowled over about a dozen in his rush and the rest scattered far and wide, leaving him in sole occupation of the playing-ground. They never badgered either of us again. He ended up by being very popular and their acknowledged leader in 'battles' against neighbouring schools.

There is also the Jews' distinction in sport to be

remembered, notably in what is perhaps the most courageous of all sports: boxing. There have been and still are many distinguished representatives of the game produced by East London Jewry.

It was probably our traditional 'minority' status that kept us in restraint. We were never allowed to forget that we were 'foreigners'. It was up to us to be on our best behaviour. Our parents continually reminded us:

'One bad Jew gets the whole race into trouble. The Gentiles don't judge us by the best, but by the worst among us.'

It seemed a queer world to us children.

We were therefore a much better behaved group than the Gentiles. We would never go as far as they did in mischief. They, seemingly, had no limit. I remember, when about eleven, cuffing the head of Billy Griggs, the younger brother of Archie, and how he quickly whipped out a penknife and stabbed me on the hand. The pain was not half so great as the shock of his action. I felt as though he had made an attempt on my life. I stared stupidly while he ran off.

The Griggs family, as a bunch, were rather typical of the worst aspects of the Gentile. From the parents down to the six-year-old girl they boozed. Occasionally the children tried to emulate the drunken exploits of their mother, whom they feared but secretly admired. She was a large, blowsy woman with heavy breasts hanging so low that she seemed in a perpetual state of pregnancy. All day she shuffled to and from the street corner in a pair of slippers. She never wore shoes. She didn't need them. Her travels took her no farther than the pub.

In spite of her physical deterioration she was still as strong as a horse, and her lean, vacant-eyed husband played second fiddle to her. Her conversational tone was a quarrelsome bawl. You didn't have to see her to know she was present in a gossiping crowd of women.

On her particularly noisy returns from the pub it wasn't

only the Jews that suffered her abuse — she dispensed it all round, sometimes including her own family. I remember being out fairly late once and passing Archie Griggs leaning up against the lamp-post at the corner.

'Can't y' get in, Archie?' I said. I thought his parents had gone off with the key.

'Naow.' He was a thin boy, with sandy hair and the pathetically vacant look of his father. His hands were thrust deep in his trousers pockets. His bare knees knocked together slightly from the cold.

'Ole woman's makin' trouble,' he muttered. He seemed puzzled rather than resentful, as if he could not understand her venting herself on him when there were so many Jews to pick on.

Sometimes Archie himself and the younger Billy acted 'the drunk', in spite of the fact that they never got more than the dregs of their parents' glasses and could not have possibly been in a state of intoxication. They would leave the pub before closing-time, taking a zigzag passage home and kicking up a general shindy in the style of their much-admired mother. They never did anything more harmful than waking up some of the children with their singing. Archie would lurch down the roadway, while Billy as the calmer influence would try to steer a straight course for him and prevent him from 'attacking' passers-by — the last thing Archie would in reality have dared do.

Every time Archie and Billy got away with a display of this kind they swaggered around for days afterwards. They felt universally feared and admired, like their mother.

I think it was the pub that represented the fundamentally different codes of our two peoples. Drink is an important element in the social life of a slum. By abstaining the Jews proclaimed their independence as a racial entity; for the Gentiles this abstinence established beyond doubt the much-talked-of miserliness of the Jew. Our people were quite unmoved by their contempt. To us they were obscene animals who squandered hard-earned money that should have been spent on their homes. Drink for us was symbolised in Mrs. Griggs and her bare-footed children.

CHAPTER 2

Religion

W E Jewish children acknowledged the superiority of the Gentile method in one field: religion. He was practically exempt. With us the Rabbi dominated one part of our lives as the school-teacher dominated the other. For four days in the week — and a good slice of Sunday — we were forced to spend the time between tea and supper cooped up in the *Kheder*, the Hebrew school. Anything less like a school you never saw. It was usually a cellar-kitchen or disused workshop where the tutor, a bearded, unkempt, smelly old man in his dotage, mumbled at you for hours on end out of a large book. You had to repeat his mumbles after him. When you mumbled wrong or took a slight rest from mumbling you received a clout across the ear. It was calculated that being mumbled at for several years would by some mysterious process turn you into an enlightened and pious Jew.

In our neighbourhood we struck it exceptionally hard with the Rabbi. He was one of the few genuine and conscientious of the breed. We considered this our misfortune. He hadn't, like most, taken up tutoring as a method of earning himself a kind of old-age pension. He was young and teaching was his Life's Work. His honesty of purpose made life a misery for us. He didn't recognise stupidity as an obstacle: he guaranteed to drum the Talmud into you at any price. And he did. When you finished his course you found you knew something of it — whatever other intentions you had started out with.

He went by the peculiarly un-Hebrew name of Rodkinson;

it had probably been given him by the immigration authorities to save tongue-twisting. We called him 'Squinty': presumably on account of the thick, black-rimmed, enormous glasses he wore. Behind them his glare was ferocious. Occasionally when he took them off to wipe the lenses you saw his eyes were really weak and you didn't fear him then. But he never kept his glasses off long enough for you to derive any permanent confidence from the knowledge.

Squinty was fortyish and thick-set, seeming even more so because of a hump that he had got himself in devotion to the Cause. His energy was tireless, his fanaticism a frightening thing. He expelled boys by the dozen. The money didn't worry him. If he could turn out a few boys that would do his teaching credit he would die happy. Our parents respected him like God.

He had rented a small, disused workshop as his *Kheder*. It was in the back-yard of a crowded tenement house, and next door to the lavatory, whose door strangers often mistook for the *Kheder* door — and vice versa. We sat on wooden forms, our books resting on plain wooden desks in front of our eyes, faced by Squinty in a chair when he took the boys individually, and standing when he conducted the chanting. A cigarette never left his mouth. He puffed at it furiously through a long cigarette-holder. Sometimes we could see only his eyes gleaming at us out of a smoke-screen.

He had an eagle eye that struck terror into the shirkers. He could also lip-read with uncanny expertness. When he suspected some one of mumbling gibberish instead of the correct text he went across and bent his ear to the boy's mouth, like a gravely attentive doctor at the chest of a patient. A few seconds was all he needed to verify his suspicions. He would raise his head and with ironic wonder announce to the four walls at large: 'So young, and already he speaks a foreign language!' The rest of us dared not lift our eyes. It was an understood thing that we were to go on with our chanting, no matter what happened at the back of the class. We merely kept our ears open for the first cries of anguish. They were not long in coming. Squinty had one method of punishment: he grasped a piece of your cheek between forefinger and thumb, pulled it as far as it would stretch, then let go and followed with a resounding smack. The number of times he did this depended on the heinousness of your offence. When he picked on somebody at the back of the class we in front could barely suppress our giggles. Especially when it was a fat boy. Squinty picked on fat boys most. He seemed to get a savage pleasure in handling them. You could see it in the tense twist of his mouth. Unquestionably there was a sadistic streak in him. Our fattest boy, 'Tubby' Beck, was his most frequent victim, although he was by no means the least attentive or most stupid among us. Squinty's aim in life seemed to be to reduce Tubby's face to a pair of cheekbones.

Squinty was a vast, ominous shadow over our lives. His influence extended far beyond the *Kheder*. When you misbehaved at home they threatened to call him in to you, just as other parents threaten you with the bogy-man. When you played football in a near-by street on a Sunday and all the neighbours' cajolery and threats failed to drive you away they went for Squinty. We prayed for the last day of *Kheder*: the day that would leave us as free as the Gentile children. We envied and admired their general disrespect for every one. A most awe-inspiring occasion was the Sunday on which our street team played a match with a Gentile street team — interrupted half-way by the arrival of Squinty, fetched by one of the tenants. We stopped our game as we saw him coming. The Gentiles gazed nonplussed at us and at him. We wondered what they would do.

As Squinty came close he waved his hand at us in a gesture of dismissal:

'C'mon, clear off 'ome, boys.' He spoke in a very Jewish accent.

Some of the Gentiles laughed.

'Gertcher, Foureyes!' one of them called.

Squinty strode forward angrily. Two of them tried to kick his shins as they backed away.

'Kick him in the ——!' yelled a voice.

We were very uncomfortable: it would all come back to us, we knew. We didn't quite like their irreverence, either. Our racial solidarity was evoked. We felt that indirectly we ourselves were being slighted.

'Let's play somewhere else,' our captain suggested awkwardly. We began to move off, to show Squinty we weren't associating ourselves with the others' defiance. The Gentiles followed us unwillingly and Squinty stood there breathing hard — the conqueror yet again.

That was the kind of despotism religion was. It no doubt explains the large-scale reduction in piety amongst the new generation of adult Jews to-day. Religion for us is bound up with memories of stuffy cellars, perpetual beatings and a brutal curbing of our childish instincts. When you left the *Kheder* after your *Barmitzvah* at the age of thirteen it took you exactly one week to forget all you had learned. The *Kheder*, constituted as it was, proved itself to be a first-class training ground for future atheists. A Squinty who was alive to-day would be stricken with grief at the outcome of his striving: like many an idealist's it was to all apparent meaning quite wasted.

CHAPTER 3

Education

T H E *Kheder* was, after all, only the counterpart to school. The method of disseminating culture was identical in both: it was based on the superiority of the cane to the text-book. Each was a miniature model of an Empire outpost.

The school discipline was of a reformatory kind. (Perhaps that is what made the reformatory itself so little feared by those boys who were threatened with it as a punishment.) The cane was constantly under our noses when not belabouring our behinds. You never saw a teacher without one under his arm. Presumably the idea was to put the fear of God into you. In this respect it succeeded as little as the *Kheder*. What it did was to make the teacher, like the Rabbi, your life-long enemy. Your one aim in life was to catch him napping.

There were more than three hundred of us in the Big Boys' section. The quota was roughly sixty to a classroom, and the number gave us confidence, if no particular academic advantage. We were all out to harass the man in front. He, in turn, working on the principle that attack is the best form of defence, perpetually harassed us. Almost anything you did outside breathing came in the category of a misdemeanour. There were no graded punishments. You got as much for surreptitiously sucking sweets as for cheeking the teacher. Consequently most of us preferred the latter pleasure as the rarer one.

The discipline was undiscerning: all were regarded as future offenders from the very first moment of entering the place. That settled one's private waverings: for the only consistent thing to do after being treated as a ruffian was to do your best to earn the title.

Of this team of disciplinarians the headmaster was the strictest. He had presumably been recommended for his post not on the strength of his knowledge, but on the strength of his arm. He liked to punish certain misdemeanours personally. Late-comers were his special meat, for they transgressed in large numbers at a time and he could fill in an interesting morning dealing with them. He punished them collectively. The same fate was meted out to those late by a minute as to those late by fifteen minutes. This encouraged late-comers to make a good job of their late-coming. He was there in the hall waiting for them every morning. They were lined up before him, and cane in hand he passed along the ranks, dealing out summary punishment. He never inquired any one's reason for being late. He acted on the principle that it was better to punish ten honest boys than to let one liar go free. The usual quota of late-comers was about forty, which made for him a fairly healthy day's exercise. They were dispatched very rapidly to their classrooms, there to demoralise the morning's lesson with their aches and groans.

There was scarcely a teacher in the school under middle age. One suspected they had spent the early part of their lives qualifying for the post as prison-warders. They had that cold, impersonal air towards their pupils that warders have to convicts in their charge.

Like warders they came off least best against the toughest characters. These were boys of an obstinate but not a disorderly kind. What they kicked against was suffering a penalty out of all accordance with the particular crime committed. They had a strong and invincible sense of justice. 'Only had a little one I wanted to finish, sir,' they would plead on being told to 'bend over' for sucking sweets in the classroom. A wise teacher would perhaps have been content to impose some lighter punishment, or a caution. But here you saw the danger of committing the power to inflict violence into unsympathetic hands. These men had no real liking for children, least of all for the slum brand. They were merely there to get through the day with as little inconvenience to themselves as possible. Unfortunately they didn't always choose the wisest method of achieving this end: it was not uncommon for a teacher to go home as badly bruised as the pupil whom he had ostensibly punished. Very often, also, a teacher would not tackle a notoriously 'tough' boy single-handed, but would fetch a couple of his colleagues to help hold down the victim, while the rest of us would look on in white-hot fury at such baseness, with some of the bolder spirits interrupting the performance with cries of 'Bastards!'

During the recess we would make plans to waylay the chief offender and after school he would make his progress to the station to the accompaniment of stones and rotten fruit flung from ambush.

One of the school's problems for a time was my elder brother. He was a wild, overgrown boy of violent whims and habits that only by sheer Providence fell short of crime. He managed to get away with it through being as brilliant as he was rough. At eleven he had already spent a year in the top standard and there was nothing more they could do with him in a classroom. He was made a monitor. This entitled him to sit all day at the headmaster's desk in the hall, looking after nothing in particular. I was very proud to see him there on the occasions I came up from the Infants' to deliver a message. School-fellows were always deferent to me when they found out he was my brother; he was reputed to be the school's 'best fighter' — a position he was continually being challenged for by other overgrown toughs like himself. It was a common experience for me to be interrupted in the midst of a game by the breathless arrival of a fellow-urchin with the news that my brother was ' 'avin' a go round the corner!' I usually arrived in time to see the brawl being broken up by the police, the teacher, or the neighbours — according to the site chosen for the battle.

My brother always came out best in these encounters, except for a regularly sprained finger, due to a whim he practised of aiming for his opponent's forehead. The explanation given at the hospital afterwards was that he had 'hit a door'. This explanation must have struck him as the last word in ingenuity, for he never varied it and the doctor was never sufficiently inquisitive to ask him the reason for this apparently long-standing and unprofitable grudge against household fittings.

In our school, as in most strictly-controlled institutions, a great deal of bullying went on unchecked among the scholars themselves. It was impossible for a youngster to avoid being a victim of it. An older boy would bear down on you during play-time, thrust his face into yours and inquire, 'Wan' a fight?' The natural retort of 'Why?' wasn't accepted as a legitimate one; it would land you in a fight whether you wanted one or not. If you said yes the same consequence followed. Only by a direct no could you escape with a few short and contemptuous blows and the slur of cowardice. For many it was the more unpleasant alternative.

The playground at school therefore, was a kind of miniature jungle where the large animals hunted the small. When I entered the Big Boys' at the age of seven I was appalled at the prospects awaiting me daily. For the first six months it wasn't so bad, especially when it got around who my brother was. But later I was alone and my only alternative was to keep out of the limelight or make a desperate fight of it with my feet if I got cornered.

At the close of the next six months, however, my brother made a short afternoon visit to the school in the role of an 'old boy', most of which time he spent careering round the playground with me perched on his back, pointing out my persecutors. One by one he hunted them down and thrashed them, with the exception of two boys who escaped by locking themselves in the lavatory. For these unsuspecting two he waited outside the school premises later — where, coming out in each other's company 'for safety's sake', they landed most conveniently in his arms and had their heads thoroughly banged together.

I lived in peace for a while, but people's memories grew short. One by one the old bullies came back at me again. By that time I had got myself some friends and together we formed ourselves into a gang with an arrangement to make a collective onslaught on any bully who attacked us singly. We called ourselves The Terrible Trio, or The Avengers, or whatever new name caught our fancy in the current weeklies. We concocted a special whistle that was intended to act as an S O S whenever one of us was in trouble somewhere. Only these precautions could make play-time bearable.

CHAPTER 4

Remember the Sabbath

As a result of spending more time cooped up indoors than
nature had intended us to we took our few pleasures with an
extraordinary degree of intensity. Like adults Saturday was
our big day. For them no work, for us no school or *Kheder*.
Unlike them we didn't lie abed late. By some curious caprice
we awoke earlier than usual just on the day that we need
never have awoken at all. My mother could never get over
this piece of childish devilry. At eight o'clock we were already
in the street kicking a ball about. We didn't kick it in our
own street. It would have meant trouble for us, being seen
by Squinty playing on the Sabbath. Strictly speaking we
were all supposed to be at the synagogue with our fathers.
And we were — those of us whose fathers attended synagogue. My own father didn't; he liked to sleep of a Saturday.
He thought he made up for it to God by sending *me* to *Kheder*
in the weekdays.

Those mornings meant a great deal to us. We had the
streets practically to ourselves, for the shops and markets
were closed and people stayed indoors. In the summer we
would spend the whole time in the swimming-bath. But even
in the winter it was good. *Any* place that was free from adults
was good.

By dinner-time we were just in the mood for the day's
high spot: the cinema. It meant all to us that it meant to
adults. Perhaps more: when *we* went to a cinema we kept
our eyes on the screen — not on the girl sitting in front of
us. *We* didn't need to pay higher prices for back seats. For

our simple and honest purpose any seat in the place was good enough.

We went there straight after dinner. It was cheaper at that time of the day and also fitted in with our parents' plans for not having us out late. We were very discriminate in our choice of cinemas. A programme had to be of a certain quality to get our support. We didn't, like adults, go merely for the sake of seeing pictures. They had to be good pictures. Nor did we wait until we were facing the screen to find this out: once you have paid your discoveries cease to have value. We made it our business to get all that information during the week. There were two elements — one negative, one positive — that we demanded in a programme: the first was 'not too much love' in the big film, the second was 'a serial' among the supporting items. With an exceptionally good serial we were prepared to compromise on the rest. The serial was the big moment in the show. If you missed an 'episode' one week you felt it to be one of the major tragedies of mankind. In the intervening days between two 'episodes' we argued heatedly among ourselves on the likelihood of the heroine, whom we had last seen trapped in a cave of slowly-rising water, drowning — or being rescued in the nick of time by the hero. It worried us a great deal.

It was a very eventful afternoon at the cinema. There was as much drama off the screen as on, due to sporadic conflicts that broke out in various parts of the hall when a porter tried to eject children who were attempting to see the show through a second time. The management had invented a system of coloured tickets to keep a check-up on this kind of thing. Maybe this was necessary in view of the habit pre-valent among children of seeing a show through twice. But the complications it brought! Children were not to be ejected easily after waiting a whole week to get inside.

One had to be thankful it was the day of the silent film: you could still enjoy yourself if you kept your eyes fixed on the screen. You had to be philosophic about other people's troubles. These only seriously disturbed you when they happened in your vicinity. It is hard to get the best out of a film when a couple of people are having a wrestling match in the next seat.

The actual physical struggle is preceded by a short, tense dialogue that is no less disturbing. It goes on these lines:

Porter: 'All red tickets out!'

Child: 'Gern — ain't seen a full show yet!'

Porter: 'You've got a red ticket — out, I said!'

Child: 'Shan't. Ain't seen the big picture!'

Porter: 'Out, I said.'

Child: 'Call me big bruvver to yer!'

Porter: 'Call your 'ole bloomin' family! Nah, then!'

Child: 'Shan't! I'll kick yer. . . .'

Porter: 'Oh, you will?'

This is where they come to grips and very shortly the porter is pushing past you, dragging in his wake a furious and kicking urchin who lands much more damage on you than on him. Afterwards you somehow have to attend to your injuries without taking your eyes from the screen. You simply can't afford to miss pieces of the show in the hope of making up for it when the programme comes round again: they may soon be along for *your* red ticket. . . .

It is true, of course, that the management was often in the wrong and you were the victim of a mistake. That didn't help. They had their system of tickets and preferred to place reliance on that than on your word. For some reason misunderstandings of this sort invariably arose when I went to the pictures with my elder brother. In the little cheap cinema we patronised some of the porters had at last learned to leave him alone, for he was a most tenacious customer to handle. But often they didn't recognise him in the dark. . . . Long after I was already out in the gangway he was still battling lustily with a couple of porters. One alone could never handle him. Two stood a better chance but failed nearly as often. He did more damage to their cinema than the trouble of throwing him out was worth. I have seen him create absolute havoc in these struggles. Once they actually got him as far as the gangway, but he caused such a panic and stampede in the queue there that several people were injured and four innocent ones ejected by mistake before they found him. In the end they would always have to let him stay. My brother rarely got any of his pleasures without a great deal of violence — but I think he preferred them that way.

The heyday of films for us was during the First World War. Even 'serials' took a back seat in our imagination beside the spectacular appeal of the 'War' pictures. These were a magnificent outlet for our pent-up spirits. It was also a means of hitting back at the Germans: during the week they had us at their mercy in air-raids, but on Saturday we went along to the pictures to witness the turning of the tables. They always came off second best in an encounter with the English in a picture. We were really there for the purpose of gloating. In every picture they did just the sort of scurvy tricks expected from the Enemy: they would capture a Belgian village and pester the innkeeper's beautiful daughter — until the arrival of the handsome English captain and his regiment. We waited for that moment in a frenzy of impatience. Coo, wouldn't those Germans cop it! And they did. It was all up with them once the English came. It was *always* all up with them when the English came. It puzzled us how the War could keep on with the Germans continually getting it in the neck like that.

But it did, as we now know. And life even for us children was a grim affair on weekdays. Only the Saturday, when it came, evened up the score and helped us face the coming week's fears with a new fortitude.

CHAPTER 5

On the Make

O u r big problem was one not exclusively childish: money. We were always conscious of its scarcity. Apart from our picture-money on Saturday and a ha'penny or penny a day during the week anything extra was a windfall — or stolen.

It obsessed us more than you might expect. Not that we had any qualms about the rent! But there were things that seemed to us as equally necessary to life and we coveted them as yearningly as adults covet fine clothes and jewellery. What made the absence of these things even more deplorable in our case was that our wants were so much simpler and cheaper than theirs — yet none the less unattainable. In the possession of 'child's property' we were as barren a bunch of paupers as you would find. In an area comprising seven or eight streets only one of us owned a three-wheeled cycle. Four or five in the same area had roller-skates or a scooter and a good round half-dozen owned a cricket-bat or a ball. The last article, incidentally, led the shortest life of any toy. One lusty kick in a football game would send it over the roof-tops for ever.

Toys were therefore at a premium. The owners of the rarer kind were the money-makers of the neighbourhood. They hired them out to the rest of us. For a ha'penny the owner of the precious three-wheeler would let you amble round the blocks for a half-hour on his machine. It was a slow, creaking affair and he made it even less exciting by insisting on being present, to see that you didn't give any of your friends a 'ride on the back'.

He was our wealthiest property-owner. People several

On the Make

streets away had heard of his cycle and came along to hire
it out. It had been given him by a visiting relative from
America a year before. From then on until the end of his
school-days he never went short of sweets — *we* went short
of them for him. He must almost have been a paying proposition to his parents. All they had to do was keep him in
clothes and food. He got the rest with his cycle.

The roller-skate and scooter owners did rather less well.
Sometimes they had to be content to hire out their property
for a bite of an apple or a dip into a bag of sweets. The
owners of cricket-bats or balls came off more poorly still.
We were well aware that a bat is of no use to anybody unless
he can get some one to bowl to him, or a ball unless he can
persuade some one to kick it with him. The price we paid
these people was our co-operation; if it happened to be a
pleasure also, then we could only wish that all payments
were so easy.

The making of money was by no means a practice
exclusive to toy-owners. Each and every one of us had a
try. There were certain well-known methods. The most consistent and established ones were the sale of cigarette cards
and second-hand magazines. Prices fluctuated according to
supply and demand: the rarer cigarette cards and magazines
were naturally the most costly. If you were the sole possessor
of the card with the photograph of Aston Villa's new All-
England centre-forward you could get a fabulous price for
him; three ha'pence perhaps. You would have to put in a
strenuous piece of haggling all the same. Nothing was ever
sold without words. The tradition of the local market was
too strong with us.

The virtue of cigarette cards was that with luck you could
enormously multiply your stock. This you did by playing a
rival card-owner at 'blowings'. You chose some one's
window-sill, placed two cards each at a time thereon and
took turns blowing at them. Whatever finished up photograph upwards was yours. Frequently one of the cards

37

blown at would sail down into the cellar-grating beneath and a knotty legal problem concerning ownership would arise. . . .

The sale of second-hand magazines was a rather less lucrative business. Here the values of the adult world were reversed. There was no such thing as a 'precious antique'; the older a thing the cheaper it was. What the smart fellow did was to buy his weekly picture-book very early on the day of publication, read it at breakfast, and sell it at school later on for seventy-five per cent of its shop price. School was the chief centre for this sort of transaction. There were three 'sheds' in our playing-ground, one of which long-established custom had reserved exclusively for the magazine pedlars. It was just like any market, except that only one kind of commodity was sold. The ritual went on traditional lines: at play-time you took up a position in there, and began chanting: 'To-day's *Magnet* — three-'a'pence. Brand-new and undamaged. Who'll buy?' As everybody almost without exception was an inveterate reader of the *Magnet* you stood a good chance of getting back seventy-five per cent of your original outlay and so having your own 'read' at the cost of only a ha'penny.

You had to use your lungs pretty strenuously amidst the noisy competition. You were spurred on the knowledge that by the afternoon your copy would be worth only a penny. Even in the morning you were never quite safe; there was always a chance of some cut-price rival beating you to it.

The real hard work started when a prospective client accosted you. You had both learned your lesson well by listening to the women at the street-barrows. The dialogue was almost identical:

'Three-'a'pence for that? Gern, it's old!'
'Old? I only got it to-day. Look at it — white as snow.'
'This corner's got a crease!'
'What difference does that make?'

'Makes it *old*. . . . Give yer a penny for it!'

'It cost *me* twice as much!'

'Take it or leave it. *I'll* find somebody who'll take a penny.'

'Betchyerwon't!'

'No? You watch me!'

'Please y'self. . . . Hey, come back! All right, take it for a penny. I'm losin' on yer. Still, you're a customer o' mine. Always makes it my policy to please a customer. . . .'

There were actually more remunerative kinds of ventures, but these unhappily were only practicable at certain seasons of the year. You could make and sell toffee-apples in the winter. Preparations for this consisted in collecting from the domestic larder in small daily portions, over a long period, a considerable load of sugar and apples. Then when mother was out shopping one day you would turn the place into a confectionery kitchen. The result, it is true, wouldn't exactly recommend itself to a sensitive palate, but the palates of small boys do not fit this description. With your outlay as nil you could afford to cut your price to a minimum. Small boys will buy anything that is cheap. Quality is of quite secondary importance.

It was only the risks attached to toffee-apple production that deterred most of us from trying. You might burn the toffee, for one thing; you might set fire to the whole house, which was rather worse. Then there was always the possibility of your mother's unexpected return. Even in the very best eventuality you would need to do quite a lot of explaining away the peculiar smell that pervaded the house for days afterwards.

The 'business' with perhaps the most lucrative possibilities of all was the trading of Spanish nuts in Passover week. Its chief drawback was its confinement to these seven days in the year: some of us felt that only this cruel whim of tradition cheated us of everlasting luxury. Meanwhile you made

the best of what you had. As with the toffee-apples there
was no outlay, for Jewish mothers habitually stock the house
with Spanish nuts in the Passover week. If you were frugal
and enterprising you could corner a market until demand
overran supply, then sell out and live in bilious luxury at the
confectioner's for a fortnight afterwards.

The way to amass stock was to play your own nuts against
other people's. There were various traditional games. One
was guessing whether the nuts in your opponent's closed fist
were of an odd or even number. Winner took all. Another
game was 'up the line': you stood in the gutter and threw
nuts up to the wall, and whoever first hit an opponent's nut
with one of his own collected the lot. There were numerous
other games, rather more intricate.

If you had a bit of 'capital' it was worth starting up on
your own. You cut five square holes in the cover of a card-
board boot-box, labelled them 8, 5, 3, 2, 1, respectively, and
invited people to have 'a nut a shy'. You offered them a
return in nuts equivalent to the number of the hole their
nut rolled into; all nuts that 'missed' were yours. It looked
like a philanthropic gesture on your part. Funfairs give the
same impression. With you, as with them, customers
invariably aimed for the highest numbers, although these
were the least accessible: you had seen to that when cutting
your holes. It hadn't taken you long to learn that the world
is full of optimists.

Of course, sometimes a skilful performer could get suc-
cessive bull's-eyes on your higher numbers, and that was the
sort of eventuality for which you needed 'capital'. The best
thing was to be able to go into partnership with somebody.
One of you would do the 'playing', and one of you the
selling. Or else both of you 'played' in different parts of the
street and met at intervals to check up on the collective
proceeds.

For seven days our street was a noisy nut market. It went

on without pause:

'Twenty-five for a ha'penny. Roll up!'

'A nut a shy — who'll buy?'

'Thirty a ha'penny — going cheap.'

'Who wants to play me? Any game, any limit!'

Passover week must have been a busman's holiday for our parents.

CHAPTER 6

Morals

UNLIKE the sheltered middle-class and upper-class children who have to get their sex values from what they read or pick up in odd places we got ours directly from life itself. When seventeen-year-old Toby Matchik was seen spending her evenings with Maxie Kalmus in the narrow alley a few doors from the pub and several months later there was talk of their getting married because of a coming child, we had a fairly true, if not quite technically correct, idea of what they'd been up to. Sex in that way became for us something associated with dark corners, something you never spoke about openly, but only hinted at by nudging and shy giggles. That seemed to be the normal attitude to it. Even at the 'mixed' central school that I attended at the age of twelve there was always an undercurrent of sexual intrigue, carried on it must be admitted, however, mostly in the form of an exchange of glances — except when one of the more 'forward' girls slipped a note across to you imploring you to look up words like *groin* in the dictionary

Sex was a problem of which the shyest of us pretended to be unaware. Recognising it was tantamount to being in the know about something dirty. In fact our term for what we imagined was the sexual act was: 'doing dirty'. When you wanted to slander some one you didn't like you got a piece of chalk and informed the world at large on some public wall that he had 'done dirty' with a certain somebody else of the opposite sex. There was nothing more shameful you could tack on to anybody.

Even if only in a subconscious way sex must have been

constantly in our minds, for life was pretty public in our street. You had only to go to the window of the top room of the house, and from there you could overlook the whole run of back-yards, including those of the houses of the adjacent street, whose yards were back-to-back with ours. You could spend a most interesting half-hour there.

Mostly you saw the same things. Women at their wash-tubs, children urinating in the middle of the yard. Sometimes, in the warm weather, a girl coming out to wash naked. Mostly it was people going to the lavatory. Very few of them closed the door. They seemed to have a strange notion that they were in the privacy of their homes and forgot the bird's-eye view.

The more 'advanced' of the boys were scarcely believed when they tried to explain the sexual act. It seemed ridiculous. It made you ashamed of your parents. You'd expected something rather more sensible from adults.

There was the shock we all got when Squinty's wife gave birth to a child rather late in life. It was their first. One had never expected it from a Rabbi and specially so pious a one as Squinty. We could only conclude that he had suc-cumbed to some evil influence.

Sex was constantly being kept in the forefront by scandals in the neighbourhood. Mostly these derived from the alley near the pub. Shovel Alley we called it. It was more like a cleft in the wall than a human habitation. There were only seven houses there, all of them down one side, facing a low, blank wall overlooking some 'ruins'. We liked to climb into the 'ruins' and prowl around the garbage for 'buried treasure' or forgotten knick-knacks. Our parents were con-tinually forbidding us to go there. They were afraid we would 'learn bad things' from the pimps, prostitutes and criminals that constituted the Alley's population. This we actually tried our best to do. We were always around their windows of an evening, which to our disgust were invariably kept shuttered and blinded — increasing our suspicions. We felt that, if we could only get a peep inside, there would be revealed to us vice of the most splendid and unprecedented kind. Sometimes we formed gangs of Vigilantes with the avowed intention of 'rounding up' the Alley denizens. But we never got to doing anything beyond inventing a password or secret sign.

The seven houses seemed to domicile countless people. You couldn't tell who was a resident and who a visitor. They all looked alike. The men were hard-faced and walked with a gangster-like slouch; the women wore hair that changed its colour with the seasons and tripped around in precariously high heels. They weren't like other women we knew. If you shouted something facetious when they passed, or threw a snowball at them in winter, they didn't squeal or hurry off discomfited, but turned round and let loose a flood of language that was a real eye-opener in the art of vituperation. We managed to pick up quite a lot of new words from them that were ultimately incorporated into our vocabulary. Mostly we steered clear of them. You never could tell what they might do. And you had the certain knowledge that there was no protection to be got from your parents; for *they* feared them too.

The Alley denizens kept to themselves — except when they quarrelled: then it spread like a conflagration. Our parents would drag us into the house so as not to hear the language. But it didn't really help. You could have heard them from inside a tomb. With the Alley denizens a row went much further than words: an ambulance as well as a policeman was necessary at its close. Often a neighbour would surprisingly find himself in the company of one of the protagonists on the way to the hospital, for flying bottles sometimes reach an unintended mark. This was the penalty for inquisitiveness.

These quarrels taught us more about sex than anything else did. For they were invariably sex quarrels: somebody had seduced somebody else's 'client', or a 'kept' male had been adding grist to his mill with strange women. There was always a woman in it somewhere. This seemed to lend the quarrel a detail of horror that no other element could.

It all went to form our opinion of women in conversation afterwards. Mostly we took the men's side. Women appeared to us as objectionable — if necessary — creatures, demanding an impossible fidelity from the male. It coloured our whole attitude to them later on in life. You grew up with the conviction that they had to be kept in their place. You needed to have them, it was true, and towards gaining this end you were justified in 'being nice' to them and deceiving them with soft words. When you had got what you wanted you didn't need to keep this up any longer. Then you treated them like the dirt they really were.

My own family was a miniature, sex-divided world on its own. We made up an equal number of boys and girls — counting out my elder brother, who was the offspring of my father's first wife. I was my mother's first child and by the time I was eight there were three others to keep me company. Childbirth seemed a commonplace occurrence in our home. There was one every two years until I reached the age of twelve — when it came to a dead stop either through sterility or economy. I always knew there was a birth when on my return from school the door was opened to me by a small, chirpy, rosy-cheeked widow from across the way called Feigele. She acted foster-mother on those occasions. 'Come in, your tea's waiting,' she would say brightly, as if she had been welcoming me from school every day of my life.

'Where's my mum?' I would falter.

She would turn her eyes briefly ceiling-wards with a finger to her lips and I was supposed to guess the rest. From then on she would bustle around the house in discreet activity, seeing to the meals and doing the things my mother did, but all the same it was like being an orphan.

After several anxious days of expectation on my part she

45

would take me by the hand one day and lead me upstairs into the bedroom. There would be some females talking animatedly round the bedside who would make way for me to take a glimpse of my 'new baby brother' (or sister). It looked the same each time, however, and I wondered what the fuss was about. I was also puzzled how it had got there. I invariably concluded they had smuggled it in during my absence at school.

I don't recall any particular significance for me in seeing it being powdered daily by the nurse later on. I believe I had a notion that the sexual organs of infants were peculiar to their kind and were not to be thought of in relation to adults' organs. My first vivid realisation of the sex-difference came from the sight of a younger sister aged four peeing in the back-yard. I remember thinking how strange the whole procedure was and not to be compared with the effortlessness of the male way, nor with its potentialities: girls couldn't play the game we often played of seeing who could go higher.

At the age of eleven I still shared a bedroom with a younger brother aged eight, while two sisters aged ten and seven respectively occupied the bedroom adjoining my parents'. My brother and I usually visited them on Saturday mornings for an hour's knock-about in their bed. We had done it for years. My parents never interfered unless we made too much noise.

One Saturday morning an unnecessarily boisterous whoop from one of my sisters brought my father into the bedroom; but instead of the expected 'Let's have a bit of quiet here!' he ordered us brusquely downstairs with the injunction 'never to come upstairs again'. He grew angry at our bewildered reluctance. My mother had followed him and over his shoulder I heard her mutter in Yiddish: 'You should have stopped this before now — boys their size, too!' I got a dim hint of the trouble and hurried away feeling hurt and vaguely ashamed. I never again felt quite natural in my sisters' company.

CHAPTER 7

Crime

QUITE naturally most of our street games were make-believe versions of real-life situations. We went in for 'crime' a lot; except that we reversed the usual position and became the law-makers instead of the law-breakers.

We were continually tracking down non-existent criminals — we were wise enough to steer clear of the real ones in the Alley. We had our own head sleuth: 'Bonk' Sorsky, a thin, bespectacled youth whose reticence we interpreted as a profound preoccupation with the problems of crime. When you got a 'clue' from somewhere you took it to Bonk. Bonk would listen attentively in the style of the Master, Sexton Blake, whose 'methods' he had adopted, and then promise to 'take it up'. That was probably the last you heard of it.

Sometimes he took it up in earnest and the 'trail' would lead to the most preposterous end. That didn't worry us. It was all practice for the big job we were one day going to pull off. Each one secretly nourished the dream of finding a short cut to fame by unmasking a gang of criminals single-handed. For this end we carefully studied the Sexton Blake series in the penny weeklies. We 'observed'. We took notes. We 'shadowed' suspicious characters — usually harmless tramps made to look villainous by a week's neglect of beard. We learned to sidle along walls in the tradition of the best detectives. We foraged in dustbins for 'evidence'; when we found a torn scrap of a letter it was part of an important communication circularised among members of a gang. I remember once finding a fragment printed with a blue

47

circle: I discovered it several years later to be the trade-mark of the Blue Circle Cement Company. At the time, however, it was a precious inner document of the 'Blue Circle Gang'. I put it straight into Bonk's hands and he promised to take it up at once. Whenever I questioned him after that he was 'looking into it', and for all I know he is still doing so.

We followed what now seem ludicrous trails. Once we harassed a local tramp for weeks, undertaking our surveillance of his movement in shifts. His resentment at being perpetually followed about by a couple of small boys we interpreted as a sure sign of guilt. We grew all the keener. Some one hit upon the idea of the tramp being in reality the head of a gang that met at night in a disused house some streets away. We prowled around the place for several evenings, peering into the broken windows and running for our lives every time we heard a rat scurry.

Eventually, I believe, the tramp left the district through our attentions.

Once in practising the Law we nearly transgressed it unforgettably. We had been in the habit of setting up tribunals to try some of our friends, as a change from hunting only imaginary criminals. The 'sentence' usually involved ten minutes' incarceration in the lavatory. For a change, on one occasion, we sentenced somebody to death. He was a plump boy with a very large behind who went by the self-explanatory nick-name of Duck's Disease. It was in his back-yard that the 'court' was sitting. He thought it a huge lark being hanged: it was the first time he had come so prominently into the limelight. We stood him on a low stool, so that his head would be within reach of a short jutting post which we were using like the branch of a tree in a lynching and put the noose in place. It was only thin string. 'Duck's Disease' was expected to break it with his weight and give us all a good laugh. Someone pulled away the stool. 'Duck's Disease's' face grew very red. He looked ever so funny to us. 'Come on, D.D.!' we urged. His eyes popped helplessly. His face began to look like an over-ripe apple. One of the boys screamed. We retreated towards the door in a panic. 'Smoky', a short, agile urchin who usually played the part of a 'general' in wars with the Gentiles, suddenly dashed forward again and began to tug madly at D.D.'s feet. We watched in horrified amazement. The string snapped with a click: D.D. fell sharply to the ground. Smoky was at his neck in a moment. We came crowding round anxiously. D.D. was sitting up and blubbering. His face was now a disarming pink. 'I'll tell my dad o' you'se,' he kept wailing.

We retreated to the door again. Smoky whispered: 'Let's give 'im a bashing and he'll forget about the hanging.' The advice had a most doubtful and diabolical flavour about it, but we were now ready to follow anyone's lead. We set upon the astounded D.D. just as he was beginning to recover. When we had once more got him to a satisfactory state of hysteria, we fled.

We stayed in the near-by tenement cellars until nightfall. Then we emerged, singly, like outlaws stealing from their lair. We made straight for our separate homes. . . .

There were woeful details in the reports we exchanged next day. Nobody had got away without a thrashing. But these transpired to have been nothing more drastic than what was imposed for any ordinary misdemeanour. We were punished 'for hitting' Duck's Disease. No word was said about a hanging.

This cured us of acting the Law for a time. We decided it was safer to play criminals. We founded 'gangs'— the Black Hand Gang was one of our most popular and enduring ones — and 'terrorised' the local population. We sent anonymous notes to people we scarcely knew, threatening vengeance. Sometimes we promised them death at the stroke of mid-night — although it was quite unlikely that any of us would be about after nine or ten. It saved us the trouble of keeping our promise.

In our zeal some occasionally forgot themselves and committed real crime. Picking pockets was the most common. We ourselves didn't call it by that name; we called it 'finding' things, and justified the act by a proverb we were very fond of that went by the title of 'Findings Keepings'. This meant that other people's property found on you was yours by right of possession.

Unfortunately this custom found no recognition in the eyes of the law and frequently some one who had 'found' something was whisked off between two policemen.

We had also our habitual criminals. Young 'Snooty' Krieger, known amongst us as Snooty the Thief, was frequently disappearing for short spells in reformatories. On his return people made a pretence of believing he had been to the country and questioned him on the kind of 'weather' he had had.

We had an amused contempt for Snooty. It wasn't for his habits that we despised him, but for his failures. He invariably got caught. For us it was the unforgivable sin. Nobody respects an unsuccessful crook. A successful one may one day become a mayor or something 'big' in the City. For the failure there is only jail. We thought it only fair. In common with the rest of the world we admired brains.

A strange case of crime was that of 'Nigger's' father. Shenker was his real name. We called him 'Nigger' because of his swarthiness. I believe some of the 'swarthiness' would have disappeared in a hot bath, but the experiment was never tried. His mother was an untidy, stocky woman who shuffled about in a pair of slippers and with her hair in permanent disarray. She always looked as if she had just emerged from a particularly violent scuffle with a neighbour. Her shrill tones were constantly in our ears. The mornings were the worst. Her living-room faced our bedroom and there was no real sleep for us after 7 a.m. That was when Mrs. Shenker started rousing her children. It was a lengthy and violent process: each child was got to the sink for his wash only after a bitter struggle. Once there — with the window invariably open — she started on them all in real earnest. It lasted until the moment that they left for school. Consequently, between the hour of seven and eight 'sleep' was for us actually a kind of fitful dozing, out of which one was periodically startled by a particularly shrill cry from across the way. To this day my mother is an incurable insomniac through such experiences. Later on, when it was necessary for her to get up at six for one of my brothers who worked at a great distance from home, she had to place the hour by other sounds. She had plenty to choose from in the slum night: it transpired that some time after dawn an old man who delivered loaves for the baker's at the corner always paused when he reached our doorstep to clear his throat noisily. The time of this occurrence coincided with the need to wake my brother. The old man has never let her down. When he dies she will probably have to buy a clock.

In those days, however, Mrs. Shenker was our clock. Though we took breakfast in the cellar-kitchen we could still hear her through the grating. We knew every one of her children's failings — Mrs. Shenker unwittingly took the whole street into her confidence:

'Jackie! Sit properly at the table — not as if you're para-lysed! I'll paralyse you for good one day . . . !'

'Sarah . . . ! Turn that pipe off and stop it running. I'll burst your head open and make *that* run!'

'Keep your hands off the loaves, Solly! A thief — that's what the boy'll grow up into. May I live so sure he will!'

This and a lot more like it was delivered in tumultuous Yiddish, interspersed with invective that no censor would permit me (and quite rightly too) to print.

It was the same rigmarole every morning. We were weary of her children's failings, we wished they would do some-thing unusual for a change — drill a large hole in the ceiling, say, or poison their father's tea. We were quite resigned to occupying the position of permanent confidante

51

to Mrs. Shenker; all we asked was a little variety.

Mr. Shenker was a man one rarely saw. He seemed a quiet, respectable sort, if a little surly in temper, but we put that down to his work and being married to Mrs. Shenker. He was a baker, and returned from work every morning to be greeted with a report on the children's behaviour. She insisted on describing every detail. Bed was denied him until he had given the children a chastisement of some sort.

We went off to school with their cries still ringing in our ears.

Later in the day we used to chaff young Nigger about the family:

'Who messed the bed last night, Nigger?' According to his mother's disclosures at the window the children took it in turns to keep her sheets in a permanent state of dampness.

'Pack it,' Nigger would say with a sheepish grin. If the chaffing was done individually he would go for the offender with a snarl. He was small and compact and could be as ferocious as a wild cat. He was much more the street-urchin than any of us. He went about barefooted a lot, like the Gentiles. The family was thought very poorly of to let Nigger do this.

It was all the more of a shock when we heard about Nigger's father. One day instead of the usual cries — which we had learned not to be alarmed at — sudden fearful screams from across the way startled us out of our chairs. When we got to the door we saw two policemen departing with Mr. Shenker between them. He was still in his working clothes. We gleaned some of the details through his wife's wailings. The rest came later and astounded us all by revealing that Mr. Shenker had been discovered using his cellar-kitchen as a coiner's den. There was a machine for manufacturing pennies. . . .

It left us gaping. We had always imagined crooks could be recognised by their social behaviour. We didn't know crime in the form in which it hid itself behind respectability.

The whole thing was a blow at our romanticism as well as our credulity.

Nigger's father disappeared for two years. The subject kept cropping up amongst us during that time. It was the details of the crime that interested us most: we couldn't get Mr. Shenker's motive in going in for pennies. Why — when one single Treasury note was worth two hundred and forty of them? We were surprised at the pettiness of his ambitions.

Outwardly things went on unchanged for the family. Mrs. Shenker resumed her daily complaints — with a little extra to make up for the threats she could no longer use against the children in the absence of their father.

Significant changes, however, had been going on behind the scenes. Mrs. Shenker soon started out to keep the family. The bakehouse where her husband had worked were kind enough to let her do occasional jobs for them delivering loaves. She also sold her own rolls in the market every day. She became a familiar sight to us, trudging the street with her large wicker basket held close.

A little later Nigger was put into an after-school-hours job. For five shillings a week he carried huge bundles of coats to the City shops daily. He hadn't much time to play with us any more.

We missed him at first. He'd been a useful centre-forward. Then it was as though he had moved to another district. Children do not yearn long for lost affections.

Sometimes we were reminded of him by the grumbles of our parents, who, when a particularly daring piece of mischief was perpetrated anonymously somewhere, thought of Nigger as the possible culprit. Except that they no longer referred to him as the 'baker's boy', but as the 'coiner's boy'. So are reputations made.

CHAPTER 8

Culture

W E didn't concern ourselves exclusively with crime in our games. Sometimes there was a kind of reaction and a short-lived epidemic of 'culture' would break out among us. We might get seized with the idea of running a magazine, or performing a play in somebody's back-yard. The first venture was the least practicable of the two. It wasn't really a co-operative effort to begin with, merely a kind of obsession that periodically took hold of me and my cousin next door and with which we infected the rest.

My cousin and I would start out with the intention of producing a magazine that was to sweep the existing ones off the market. We hadn't the faintest notion how to tackle the thing technically. We merely believed in the principle of the idea and waited for the details to suggest themselves. Which they did in a confused sort of way:

It was arranged that I would supply the 'stories'; my cousin the 'jokes'; some one else the 'articles'. We believed that these three ingredients, mixed and stirred, *must* result in a 'magazine'.

On the technical side we had to be content with doing the 'printing' on ordinary exercise-book paper, by hand, with pencils. The whole thing in fact would be a kind of home-work on a large scale — but performed with a zeal that no school home-work could ever extract from us.

We took it in turns to lend each other's homes for the work. Office-hours were between supper-time and bed and all of Sunday. We had a lot to put up with from our families, but nothing could daunt us, and when necessary we were even prepared to transfer our 'premises' to the bedroom.

We scribbled away like frantic editors trying to get the paper ready for the night mail. At the end of a week there were two copies of the 'magazine' completed. We scrutinised them proudly. The contents, I suppose I need scarcely mention, were seventy-five per cent filched from the current weeklies; what was 'original' was sheer gibberish. I remember my own 'stories', populated with numerous heroes and villains. They were full of sentences running in this style:

' *You Demon,*' *he snarled, and with a hoarse cry lurched forward* . . .

They were tales of fearful violence and people were murdered over and over again, with a contemptuous disregard of the law of mortality.

By the end of another week we had managed to produce one more copy of the magazine. Our zeal was on the wane. It was a sacrifice of labour out of all proportion to the result. With the money expended on pencils we could have kept ourselves in confectionery for a month.

We eyed the three magazines doubtfully. I suppose we were all thinking of the work yet to be done. A new-found respect for editors was born in us. One of our Committee resigned on the spot. Two others soon followed him. There were left only my cousin and me. We two persevered for another week— producing a spidery, illegible and incredibly soiled copy, due to being harried from kitchen to bedroom and from bedroom to kitchen by irate parents.

With these four copies in hand we decided to sell out and close shop. But our humiliation was not yet over; nobody would buy them. Under our very eyes friends of ours marched into the newsagent's to purchase what they termed 'the real thing'.

Eventually and only at a great loss of personal dignity we succeeded in parking three of the four copies on our respective parents at tuppence apiece. They thought it a cheap price for peace in the home; and destroyed the copies immediately on buying them. They didn't even have the grace to do it secretly. . . .

With the sixpence to comfort us in our sorrow we made straight for the confectioner's, where for two hours we sat munching desperately, like a couple of ruined financiers having their last meal. We kept the fourth copy of the magazine as a keepsake. We had a vague idea of saving it for posterity to cherish. Fortunately for posterity it was lost very soon afterwards.

Our ventures in the field of the 'theatre' were rather more satisfying. I must make it clear that in saying 'we' I am not implying that this idea, any more than the other, was a co-operative effort. In its own way it was even more of a one-man show. The brains behind this particular scheme was Ginger Sorsky, who was our left-hand neighbour and brother of Bonk. There was quite definitely a talent for the spectacular in that family. There were two more brothers, each of whom could do something nobody else could. One, I believe, could walk the length of the street on his hands, or something inhumanly acrobatic like that.

For Ginger, in the warm weather, there was only 'acting'. He was a stocky, tousle-headed, rather quarrelsome boy with a knack of talking you into things. He would get you enthusiastic against your will. Then he would launch a 'play'. Rehearsals took place in the back-yard on the occasions his mother was out shopping. Ginger didn't sit down to write a play: he made it up as he went along. It had no special ending either; it stopped at the point when Ginger could think of no new ideas. The whole thing would be a series of disconnected scenes, each one giving Ginger the chance to act as Hero. The rest of us were merely there to fit in with his personal plans. We were really kind of extras. Ginger was the star. He went through danger-fraught situations, laying low numerous 'villains' in turn, and emerging unscathed and triumphant at the end.

The play was modelled on the current serial we happened to be following up at the pictures and characters were correspondingly titled. Sometimes Ginger was Two-Gun Pete, sometimes One-Punch Red the Ranger. Villains were invariably called Jake, or Snaky Joe. Ginger chose his cast according to his affections; his brother Bonk was usually allowed to be a kind of second 'lead', or a faithful brother, as he was in real life. The rest of us had to be content with what we got. It was a privilege to get into the troupe at all. As well as the 'honour' it meant you didn't pay for the performance. These also took place in Ginger's back-yard, for it was the largest — not in a strictly topographical sense, but in being less cluttered up with domestic bric-à-brac than most. The 'theatre' was a very democratic one. There were no graded prices. Admission was a ha'penny per person and all profits went to Ginger. To make sure of this he acted as doorkeeper before the show started.

The play always started off with a swing. Ginger worked very hard for his money. He repeatedly got himself tied to the wooden post that supported the shed in the corner and unravelled himself in time to turn the tables on his captors. From our places on the ground we looked on fascinated. Ginger was always worth our ha'pennies.

He did not always give us 'drama'. Sometimes he played tragedy. Ginger felt he had a kind of flair for it. He would betray on these occasions a surprisingly sentimental streak. He liked to avenge a murdered father. When Ginger took an oath to 'get' the assassin we felt it was all over bar the funeral.

Unluckily he often overdid it. In one play he had to kneel by the form of his prostrate 'father' and, tearing at his hair, cry in heart-rending tones:

Father — I swear reve-e-nge!

When he did it we all laughed. We weren't convinced at all. We had a feeling that Ginger had put in that bit to give him a pretext for scratching his head: he had a rather shady reputation in this sphere of hygiene.

But on the whole we enjoyed ourselves. I think this was proved by our readiness to part with what was for some of us several days' toffee money. Sometimes those of us who were rejected 'extras' took revenge on Ginger by trying to get a free peep through cracks in the fence of our back-yard. Ginger always spotted you, no matter how absorbed in his part — and would interrupt the show with some unrehearsed lines of abuse.

There was only one real trouble we couldn't surmount: that was Ginger's mother returning before schedule and chasing us all out with a broom-handle. Sometimes there was a suspicion that Ginger welcomed this event through being unable to bring his play to a satisfactory end. True, this was by no means a satisfactory end; but it was an end. Ginger's mother saw to that.

These setbacks were followed by a lull of despondency. We brooded on the petty restrictions to our exuberance. We racked our heads to devise games that would not involve a clash with parental or municipal authority. In the absence of playing-fields it was really a dilemma. We had to resort to the most pathetically repetitive forms of entertainment: there was a urinal in the next street around which we chased each other in a game of 'Touch' when there was nothing better to do — much to the annoyance of its occupants. We called the place The Green Man, in parody of a public-house. 'What about a game at The Green Man to-night?' some one would suggest.

At other times we went looking for 'lovers'. This involved peering into back turnings and shouting to the couples we imagined were sheltering in its crannies: 'Hoi, you — come out o' there!' — then dash away.

There was always a kind of half-heartedness about doing this. We were afraid we might come upon some terrible scene. We vaguely associated love-making with terrible scenes due to our experience of Shovel Alley.

Once, on creeping through a street, low, quarrelsome

voices from somewhere near stopped us short. 'Gee!' said one of the boys. It was the first time we had heard anything of the sort outside Shovel Alley. We listened.

The woman's tone gradually overrode the man's. It had a kind of restrained fury:

'. . . You shan't, d'ye hear? You just stop your poncing — or I'll have your eyes out! . . .'

'Coo!' whispered Ginger. 'She's swearing.' We hadn't somehow expected this from real 'lovers'.

'What's poncing?' asked young Benny Michaels, who was only eleven.

Nobody enlightened him. Some of us began to move off awkwardly. The more inquisitive ones soon had to follow so as not to give themselves away.

'Women,' said Ginger bitterly. The rest of us nodded in understanding.

CHAPTER 9

A Man's World

I F school life can be said to have been characterised by our ingenuity in snatching freedom under the eyes of disapproving authority, then our early working life was chiefly remarkable in ending all this. Childhood remained, but childhood habits disappeared. Working life absorbed us completely.

We had never before been so finally and utterly cornered. In spite of all, we had still succeeded, while at school, in living something of a child's life. When we were chased out of Ginger's back-yard we tried to get hold of another — or waited until the next time Ginger's mother was out shopping. When a policeman interrupted our football game we migrated to a different 'pitch'. When the owner of the 'ruins' had its walls bordered with broken glass we went exploring for fresh 'ruins'. In other words, a doggedly pursuing fate could put us down but not 'out'. There were still those rare moments when we came into our own as children.

What is strange and rather shocking in its way is the abruptness with which this ended on the day you left school. To say that it was inevitable — that leaving school at the age of fourteen implied that you were no longer a child with a child's instincts, is unconvincing. You do not change your nature over-night. Yet that is what you were expected to do.

The 'sweat-shop' was supposed to clinch the matter. For anything more discouraging to the free play of a child's instincts it would be hard to conceive. In there you were supposed to find your manhood. Working for twelve hours daily in a back room under the constant glare of an electric light, in an atmosphere that was thick with cigarette-smoke and the dust raised by treadle-machines, a room inhabited by people with crooked bodies and crooked minds, whose language was of a kind unheard of in any schoolroom and in no way toned down in consideration of a child's presence — here, by some paradoxical process, you were supposed to grow up into a fine, respectable citizen and a credit to the nation. Yet people claim to be shocked at the offshoots of the ghetto. A humane society — if such a society is compatible with the existence of a ghetto — would pin a medal on the breast of every one of its survivors.

The change-over from school to workshop is a nightmare of suddenness. It is true you may be still wearing school clothes — I didn't get my long trousers until I had earned them — but if your clothes are childish your mind is no longer so after the first day. You are serious, like a grown-up. You have seen things. You have much to ponder. Nothing experienced at school has prepared you for it; in fact, after the first day in a 'sweat-shop' you tend to be condescending about your school, even if secretly rather wretched. It has no real connection with life as you now know it. It is, you realise, a larger sort of nursery. There grows on you the conviction that school, with all its discipline, boredom and beatings, marks the end of life's happiest period. You have a feeling you will never see its like again.

Among the many changes that this first day at work brings into sharp light is the fundamental rift between you and your parents. It comes home to you how little understanding there is between you. They see nothing unnatural in a child of fourteen going out to work: they have done nothing else since infancy. They consider you lucky in having got an 'education'. You can never make it clear that just this 'education' is what has mentally conditioned you for another sort of life: it has been an education conducted on the assumption that there is a field-marshal's baton in every recruit's knapsack.

Now it seems as though for several years you have been the victim of a huge hoax. Your parents' emigration emerges as a waste of valuable time and money. They might as well have stayed where they were. You are no better off than they thirty years ago. If your father had spent his life sitting cross-legged in a Russian workshop you weren't much better off doing the same in an English one. If he had hawked fruit round the back streets there, it was not more profitable doing it here. If he had, in short, passed most of his life in a European ghetto, everything pointed to the probability of your duplicating his existence in an English one. History was a monotonous cycle. The only 'change' was in your respective attitudes: he was inured to his fate; while you would have to suffer a slow, back-breaking readjustment before you acquired his tragic and age-long resignation.

The first step in this process of readjustment is the attempt to collect some of the fragments of your young shattered life. For shattered it is. You are suddenly without recreations or friends. You do make some effort to preserve your schoolboy contacts, but everything works against it. You and they have lost the things you had in common. When you are free to take a walk in the evening it is just about your friends' bed-time. Even if the more faithful of them do concede to visit you of an evening you do not find the old joy in their company. Their talk bores you. You find the school's domestic affairs a little unreal, trivial. You no longer share their views on what constitutes having fun: kicking people's doors and running away seems to you an unprofitable form of entertainment after a day's work.

The drift away from them is rapid. In a blind, instinctive sort of way you seek others closer your own standard. The nearest thing is 'Joe's', the confectioner's at the top of the street, where the local youths assemble of an evening. You stroll along there the first time you are able to raise your tired body from the table.

You hang around the outskirts of the group, unobtrusively. They are lolling on the window outside, for it is spring. They are most of them older than yourself, men-of-the-world of sixteen, and this is the way they use their leisure. Their talk is about girls and sport. You feel very grown-up standing there with them. They don't resent you; they don't notice you. They are full of themselves.

Their subject-matter would have been a trifle above you a month ago. But the workshop has been enlightening: you follow them fairly easily.

'Stinky' Mason is the hero of this society. He is a short, pudgy youth with a pimply skin that his friends claim proudly is a consequence of masturbation. His thumbs are perpetually in his waistcoat, like a prosperous bookmaker. He is very sophisticated. He talks about 'tarts' with a bored air and is especially fond of airing his opinions on venereal disease. It is common knowledge that he has personally experienced a 'packet', so his views are authentic. He gives a horrible and incredible description of the things you are likely to contract by consorting with women. You can hardly believe it. It puzzles you why people should take the risk. To your childish, unawakened feelings they seem penalties out of all proportion to the promised joy.

When Stinky is not on 'tarts' he is voluble on sport. He hints at being in the know about every important boxing or football contest. His criticism of famous athletes is impressive, although he has never done a half-hour's exercise himself. He implies an intimacy with important figures in the sporting world:

'. . . "Listen," I says to him in the dressing-room afterwards, "you may be Kid Billings, but you'll never be champion if y' keep leavin' yourself as open as a gate! And why didn't you poke your left out more, y' mug? You'd have had him groggy in no time. You ain't usin' your 'ead, Kid," I says to him — "no, nothing like you oughter. . . ." '

We listened, awe-struck. This was LIFE.

Instinctively the younger ones amongst us gravitated towards each other. People like Stinky were very interesting in their own way, but they grabbed all the limelight. We needed equals to spend our time with.

There were four or five of us who soon found ourselves drawn together by a common age. We would take strolls, or form our own group beneath the lamp-post opposite Joe's. Ginger Sorsky was one of the bunch. He had left school only a fortnight after me.

The eldest of us was Sol Levine. He was fifteen and earned twelve-and-sixpence a week. He could inhale smoke. The rest of us couldn't even afford a cigarette.

Sol knew the West End. He took three of us along there with him on a Saturday night. We walked all the way. Sol stopped before the Coliseum and exhibited it to us as if it was his own handiwork.

He led us with a knowledgeable I-could-find-my-way-blindfold-through-here air through the back-streets of Piccadilly. He pointed out the prostitutes. He intended to 'try' one when he earned sufficient money. His brother 'had' one a week, he boasted.

'Coo!' We wondered how he had the pluck.

'Might get himself a packet,' suggested Ginger with a knowing air.

'S'right.' There was a unanimous and rather grave agreement on that. Actually, we didn't quite perceive what he might 'get', in spite of Stinky Mason's instructive efforts. We merely associated women with disease.

'Oh, you get over it,' said Sol airily. 'It's all in the game, y' know.' He shrugged his shoulders with the air of one prepared to risk his life on the toss of a coin.

'S'right,' we chorused again, if a little less confidently. A Man's life was worth all the risks. Each of us took silent dedication to it in that moment.

CHAPTER 10

The Sex Hunt

SHARING an 'understanding' of that sort there was no more need for subterfuge and pretence about sex. We made for it full steam ahead. Except that in our case methods were toned down in accordance with the restrictions. We obviously couldn't afford to haunt Piccadilly; but we could haunt the Whitechapel Road. It cost nothing to stroll along this broad promenade on the look-out for 'tarts'. You rarely did it in less than pairs. You could give each other confidence in that way for what was probably your first deliberate attempt at making sex contact. It was unwise to tackle other than your own exact number. If three girls came along and you were only two it was best to gulp down your disappointment and let them pass. Contact was made by sidling up to a group of girls coming from the opposite direction and persuading one of your number to nudge the nearest of theirs. You based your subsequent actions on the response to this. . . . Sometimes your luck was out all evening. In the desperation this brought you to, you would throw etiquette to the winds and resolve to make sure next time by confronting the girls in the fashion of an ultimatum.

Sol Levine was our best 'chatter'. He was a weedy youth with 'padded' shoulders and a swagger on the style of an American gunman. We always let him do the talking. He would open up with: 'Hallo, babes,' or 'Hallo, sweethearts,' — according to which film star happened to be influencing him at the time. (When the talkies arrived all girls were 'Honey'.) The rest of us would support him with imbecile grins.

Sol amiably tapped the nearest girl on the shoulder.

'How about you and me for a stroll, sister?'

The girl would make a pretence of contempt:

'Walk? With you? Not 'arf I would. Seen better things crawl out o' cheese!'

Sol was unperturbed. He knew the conversation had to travel along certain traditional lines.

'Me?' He affected an amused astonishment. 'J'ear that, boys? She's talking about me. Me!'

We grinned back, dutifully.

'Say, sister, if you was to know who I am — tell her, boys!' He held up a restraining hand: 'No! Why should I boast? Sol Levine doesn't have to boast.' He had got into the habit of talking about himself in the third person since reading of a character doing it in a Wild West story.

'Well, who are yer?' said one of the girls, pretending to take him seriously.

'Ol' Mother Riley!' cut in one of her friends. The rest went into giggles of laughter. Sol joined them simultaneously, apeing them in a feminine falsetto.

'Oo, I never did! I'll bust my sides in a minute, I know I shall. Oo, you cats!' He clapped everybody on the shoulder with an indiscriminate familiarity.

That did it. We were soon all talking animatedly on Sol's style. It wasn't long before we paired off for a stroll. Sol had the best girl, of course.

The Whitechapel Road was regarded as a kind of open-air brothel by some parents and all the municipal busybodies. Going there for a stroll was your first step along the road to perdition. Yet there were rendezvous more harmful. The Whitechapel Road was at least an open thing: there wasn't much you could do there with the world's eyes on you — it was probably the reason why you tried to inveigle any girl you found there 'round the back'.

The streets behind were really much more of a 'danger', looked at from the parents' view. There was scarcely one whose nooks and doorways were not seething with amorphous shadows and sporadic whisperings. In our own locality, had we decided to remain there, were the tenement cellars in the street adjacent to ours — perhaps the most notorious hang-out of all. We had used it for hide-and-seek when we were younger. Now it served for a more sophisticated form of entertainment. Young local bloods seduced girls down there. Prostitutes brought along their clients, on account of it being cheaper than a hired room. Ordinary respectable couples shunned the place: one of the open landings upstairs would do until marriage. It was understood that the cellars were not for cuddling but for the 'real thing'. To be seen entering there meant a ruined reputation — if you were a girl. For a youth it meant a step up in the social ladder. There was nothing so respected as 'experience' — what kind of experience it didn't matter.

Stinky Mason, when he wasn't at Joe's, was usually suspected of being 'somewhere in the cellars'. Once, at the suggestion of a mischievous wit, we marched in a bunch round the railings that bordered the tenements on four sides, and one of us called down at every few yards:

'Are y' down there, Stinky? Hey, watch him, Girly!'

Naturally we got no response. But we knew he'd been there, for he had a suspicious and belligerent look in his eye the next evening at Joe's; and he was very reticent. . . .

There was another, although not so widespread, method of getting sexual experience. This was at professional hands. It needed, however, more money and courage than most of us could muster and was almost exclusively the preserve of the older boys.

For a half-crown you could get 'a load off your mind' at Fat Emmy's round the corner. You could also get other things there if your luck was out: it was here Stinky was said to have got his 'packet'. Fat Emmy was the head of a coterie of middle-aged prostitutes who exploited the sexual curiosity of young boys as a side-line. Their existence was never in jeopardy thanks to the fertile ranks of the inquisitive.

For those who couldn't afford Emmy and were out of luck with the tenements there was still another source: the shilling-a-time prostitutes who worked the back streets. They were about in all weather, like stray, mangy cats. Most popular centre for their activities was a spot known as 'under the arches'. It was a street lined with warehouses on either side and as still as a cemetery when they closed down for the day: in two parts of it trains ran overhead and in the dark shelter beneath the prostitutes took their clients for a minute's joy. You didn't boast about visiting this place as you did the brothel. Even by Welk Street standards it was below par. It was considered an outlet for sex rather than an indulgence in it.

The happy medium for most, when attainable, was the domestic servants. They were pouring in from the derelict mining areas of Wales. They were young, lonely, inexperienced and simple in their needs. Their idea of a 'good time' was the pauper's dream: all one had to do was find picture money for two and it would be relatively easy to persuade them later on to take their 'Good night' in the tenement cellars. You could claim the solitude there was much more conducive to 'talking'. Once in the place the rest was easy.

Some of the boys used to entice a girl into the house when their parents were out. You had to be on friendly terms with her to make such a proposal and her own place had to be near-by so that she could return before her absence was noted. Once when Stinky Mason had achieved this on a Saturday morning after angling for it for months on end and was safely ensconced with the girl in his bedroom, some one dashed round to the synagogue to inform his father.

We didn't see Stinky for a whole week afterwards.

CHAPTER II

The Tough Life

OUR 'interests' were soon expanding. That is not to say we found different things to do; but rather did the old things with a difference. Parading the Whitechapel Road night after night was, after all, 'kid's' stuff. We gave a variation to the sex hunt: this took the form of the dance hall on Saturday night. It was a gratifying change from the perpetual importuning in the Whitechapel Road. Here you were, as a male and potential 'partner', at a premium. It was an exciting reversal of roles. Instead of casting hopelessly yearning glances at desirable but inaccessible females, you now went boldly and confidently for your choice. Any girl in the place was yours provided you could dance. It was up to you. As an added inducement there was the knowledge that any girl you danced with could be escorted home afterwards and cuddled for an hour or so in some back turning.

The week-ends were the high peaks. At each one a different girl. It was also a method of gaining an extensive acquaintance with the topography of the district, if you chose to look at it like that. Many of us learned to know the back turnings as well as the prostitutes for whom it was a professional duty.

On each Sunday following a dance we met at Joe's after a late breakfast to discuss the previous night's fun. We inquired sympathetically into each other's 'luck'. Each insisted on the superior physical attributes of his own partner. You never heard a complaint: it would have implied the possession of an inferior brand of sex-appeal. There *was* some grumbling, but it was of a facetious sort and came from people with so high a reputation for 'successes' that it implicitly flattered rather than discredited them. Sol Levine, for instance, talked of being haunted by 'bad luck' that derived from an extraneous and uncontrollable source: he invariably discovered his partner to be living in a tenement. He agreed it was a promising beginning. The snag lay, however, in these tenements always turning out to be of the smaller kind whose gates were locked at midnight, and whose inhabitants made it a strict dictum for their daughters to be indoors on time: with the consequence that Sol continually found himself having to take a hurried parting at the very moment when his spirits were at their liveliest. . . .

Attending dances regularly had its disadvantages: you were liable to be thought soft and labelled 'dancing boy'. To avoid this danger it was best to supplement your dancing with pursuits of a more 'manly' kind. That was where the billiard saloon came in. You couldn't be thought soft spending your nights there: it was the hangout of the roughest and toughest.

Our favourite was two minutes distant. It called itself The Balview Temperance and Social Club, but it was just a billiard hall. You entered it by swing-doors from the street. It was a large, square room, filled with rows upon rows of green-covered tables, except for a canteen at the far end and two or three small card-tables dotted around. The walls were distempered and crowded on all four sides with photographs of sporting celebrities. High above all was a small dusty notice — *Gambling is Prohibited* — that you didn't discover until your umpteenth visit and then only if you possessed exceptionally good eyesight. The notice had to be there by law. But the forsaken corner chosen for it showed that the proprietors had their own method of combating authority.

The habitués fitted in well with the setting. You might have thought it had been designed with their connivance and even supervision. They were as tough as anything depicted in American gangster films except that they didn't carry guns. They were none the less armed for that.

Experience had taught them that razors are quite as effective as guns and far less noisy.

We were a little 'out of it' on our first visit. Most of the occupants were well acquainted with each other and con-sorted in cliques, or gangs. This didn't necessarily involve rivalry. It was merely the division of groups with separate interests. Those who 'did' the racecourses for a living bunched together; as did the promoters of graft in the professional boxing business and the petty thieves who exchanged 'tips'. The whole was an unconscious parody of the medieval trade guilds.

Quarrels of a sort only broke out occasionally. These were exclusively between gangs who worked the same racket, one of whom had been infringing the other's ground. There was no drawing-room finesse about these quarrels. Word play was almost entirely absent or cut down to a monosyllabic minimum. *Violence* was the watchword. It reminded me of those childhood brawls in Shovel Alley. You had hardly a moment to make yourself scarce before you were caught up in a shambles: razors flashed, lights were fused — and people were trampling you down on their way to the doors.

After this initiation into the habits of the saloon 'boys' we devised our own method of protection. It became a strict point to choose the table for our own game as near the exit as possible.

You soon learned who were most to be feared. They were easy to memorise once they had been pointed out. Usually it was those with the most badly-gashed faces. The saloon 'boys' collected razor wounds with the same pride that the old Heidelberg students collected sabre cuts from their duels. These were reputedly the most reckless. Nobody cared to risk a private quarrel with them — not even the 'pugs' who sometimes came in for a game: for what use are fists, no matter how scientifically manipulated, against one who can use a razor with the ease and dexterity of a surgeon? You had proof of this in the kind of casualties the 'razor boys' inflicted. They never killed anybody outright. They knew with uncanny exactness how to time a swift stroke that scarcely skimmed your face but kept you indoors for a month.

Youngsters like ourselves, with no particular 'racket', found we had least to fear from the razor toughs. They were very carefree and jovial when not discussing a 'scheme'. We grew ever more friendly with them — in the tentative way you get friendly with a lion. They were unusually generous. Anyone 'in trouble' always found in them a ready ear. Beggars who dropped in never departed empty-handed. As for a caller on behalf of a 'deserving charity' he never had to do any collecting at all: a couple of the 'boys' would go round the place for him and bring him back a heavily-rattling box within five minutes.

When in funds they were childishly expansive. Making a 'packet' at the racecourse or doing a 'good job' in a less lawful quarter filled them with an exuberance that had to find its outlet in munificence. They would 'treat' any and every stranger who crossed their path. Most marked of all was the pity they showed for a vagrant 'down on his luck', especially if he turned out to be a 'Yiddisher boy': this touched them almost to the point of tears — these profligates who had outraged and renounced every respectable dictum of Jewry.

They undoubtedly had a sneaking regard for the under-dog. They were themselves under-dogs in a complex sort of way. There was scarcely one who hadn't been disowned by his relatives. You could call them the 'untouchables' of East End Jewry: crime and its uncertainties had enticed them from the 'safety' of drab respectability. They were unconscious anarchists. Each man for himself, was their motto, and all hands against society. Amongst God-fearing Jews their names were mentioned only in the most opprobious terms. They had put themselves outside the family; and the family for Jews is a sacred unit: it is the one element they have managed to preserve and keep intact amid the slow, advancing disintegration of the race.

The 'boys' testified in every action to the accuracy of this diagnosis. They were the most cynical set of people you were likely to meet anywhere. They scorned anything that was foreign to their own particular code of living. Something 'different' that caught their eye in a stranger at the 'hall' would lead to chaff of the most overbearing kind. They mimicked and derided anything that wasn't like themselves. And they had an almost Olympian contempt for fellow humans: if when they lolled outside the billiard hall in the warm weather a neighbour complained about their 'language', they would turn and abuse her almost to the point of violence.

They were like a strange, wild rabble let loose in an ordered society — but they revealed one trait that showed their intrinsic affinity with that society. This was an odd reverence for the elderly. If an old Jew crossed their path and scolded them, they held their mouths — no matter the provocation. This was the one childhood instinct they had never been able to eradicate. Abuse of the very elderly is for Jews a sin no amount of penance can redeem. I suppose it is a heritage from the old days of the Patriarchs. I have rarely seen this dictum broken. On the occasion it was you expected to see the offender struck down by an unseen hand in his tracks. He was certainly considered beyond redemption. Reverence for the elderly was the one thing we as children preserved in the face of all our other tattered values.

The saloon 'boys', like other Jews, are perhaps more shocked when they read of an old Jew in Germany having his beard pulled in the street than by some of the larger atrocities: these history has taught the Jew to expect. But the former strikes at the very roots of our traditional dignity. It will be remembered against the Nazis when their other crimes have faded from the records.

At this age the racial difference was becoming a distinct

cleavage. Jew and Gentile weren't sharing certain experiences any more, as in childhood. Adult standards had begun to prevail. This does not mean that our habits became fundamentally inimical. No; we merely did things with our own sort of people and in our own choice of places. Both groups haunted billiard halls, for instance; but in separate spheres. It was the same with dance halls. Our favourite was the People's Palace in Mile End; the Gentiles preferred theirs in places like the Elephant and Castle — where the presence of one of our people would be sure eventually to provoke a 'rough-house'. The Gentiles didn't like us dancing with 'their' girls. A Jew seemed always able to attract a Gentile girl more easily than her co-religionist. The same was rarely apparent in the reverse; it is probably the reason why the Jews didn't resent an occasional Gentile in their dance-hall: they knew he would have a thin time of it. A Jew, however, attending one of their halls would, by a combination of good dancing, cheek, and sexual aggressiveness walk home with the most attractive girl in the place — if they let him get that far.

It was only in the sphere of sport that the racial ratio evened itself up. Football stadiums and boxing-halls have always been international. Racial consideration, however, cropped up in the latter field whenever a Jew opposed a Gentile, making it certain that, whoever finally triumphed in the ring, the real battle would be fought out in the stalls afterwards.

Only one thing could supersede racial pride: that was local pride. It occurred when young Archie Griggs blossomed out as a pugilist. To Jew and Gentile alike he was a 'Welk Street boy'. We were his indiscriminate fans. It was true that we underwent a bit of conscience-wrangling when he was matched with a Jew, but local loyalties always triumphed over racial ones in the end. They were more valuable to us in our daily life.

We were very proud of him. We got him to join us in

jaunts to the billiard hall and people there called out 'Hiya, Archie!' although they were strangers. They came and watched when we played. We felt consciously tougher, as if with his presence we shared some of his prowess. We handled our cues like bored, sullen gangsters and looked round aggressively after each hit. We were almost in the mind to start a 'rough-house'.

CHAPTER 12

The Reward of Endeavour

WE didn't monopolise Archie for long. He was bound to fall into more important hands. Stinky Mason began paying him attention. Stinky was one of those people who, though in no way gifted themselves have a knack of playing upon the susceptibilities of those who are. He was a year and a half older than Archie and Archie was obviously as flattered to be in his company as he was to be in Archie's. They were a queer sight out. Archie with his gawky boy's figure looked the completely helpless dupe beside the short but maturely built and self-confident Stinky. When they had their heads together you felt that Stinky was instructing Archie in some particularly nasty piece of crookery.

Stinky openly regarded himself as Archie's adviser. He was for ever explaining 'the lay of things' — only stopping short at the point of demonstrating his teachings inside a boxing-ring. He knew what he was about in confining himself to word-play. Stinky was one of those people who can put up a wonderful performance from the gallery. I don't believe he had ever donned a pair of boxing-gloves in his life; his reputation rested on a record of terrorism in his schooldays and one for verbosity afterwards. The last went down particularly well at the street corner. Anything to the contrary was never interpreted as modesty, but as timidity — unless you disproved it by spectacularly beating up a bully. Your quietness even then, although respected, would still puzzle people.

Stinky now talked one subject: Archie. He had accompanied Archie to the 'gym' and he discoursed on the notabilities he had seen training there. Each occupied a separate pigeon-hole in his mind. He talked about them in the way a punter talks about horses. He was fond of discerning potential weaknesses that would be their ultimate undoing. 'His *legs*,' he would say thoughtfully about a certain boxer, pursing his lips like a doctor fearing trouble for a patient twenty years ahead. 'Of course, he's all right now doing only twelve-rounders. Twelve rounds!' He shrugged contemptuously, leaving the implications to us. Listening to him you could almost believe that twelve rounds of boxing was a trifling demand upon stamina, in spite of a previous conviction that a mere sprint up the street would have meant for people like Stinky a month's convalescence.

Stinky had free entrance to all Archie's performances. We had to queue up at the gallery. We would wait there an hour before admission time, watching the various 'personalities' arrive. Stinky swaggered up at the side of Archie, nodding affably in all directions, obviously under the impression that he was being taken for a promoter. He pretended not to hear when some one shouted across: 'Wotcho, Stinky!' — but quickened his pace noticeably.

Archie's contests took place at the Arena. It had been many things in its time, including a short spell as a Yiddish theatre. Now it billed pugilists instead of actors on the hoardings.

There were three entrances along the front, each supervised by a man who wore headgear that was meant to symbolise the kind of patron expected: the gallery man wore a cap, the one at the pit a trilby, and the one at the stalls a top-hat.

Urchins clustered near the gutter and in awed whispers asked each other the identity of important arrivals. Sometimes an intrepid one would make a dash forward and plead: 'Take us in wiv yer, guv'ner. Ain't never seen a fight.' This was the signal for one of the door-keepers to set chase to the lot.

Inside, the arc-lights revealed tobacco-smoke moving in an endless mist across the hall. The 'gallery' consisted of two rows of wooden stairs, arranged in the shape of a C all round the stalls, and divided from them by a low fence and narrow pathway. There was an air of almost unbearable expectancy; it must have been something like that at public executions. When the performers entered the ring every one stood up and remained standing. It was one roar of bedlam from start to finish. Little timid men who looked as though they suffered under a perpetual domestic tyranny shouted themselves hoarse for blood. There was scarcely one amongst that audience who struck one as ever having stripped in a gymnasium. Yet this was a section of 'our great sporting public'. It doesn't take one long to realise how small is the number of boxing fans who care two hoots about the sport as a sport. Too many are blustering weaklings who pay their money to see blood flow. They have little appreciation of a skilled performance that does not end in butchery. The real sport-lovers are to be found not among them, but among the less-trumpeted amateurs; there a man can leave a ring sound in limb without evoking the violence of the mob.

The Arena was Archie's 'public'. For the most part it was local, although a good sprinkling originated from places like Poplar, Bermondsey and Camberwell. Archie had now reached the stage of being pointed at in the street. Men three times his age tried to catch his nod. He was discussed in local sporting circles as fervently if not as frequently as Jack Dempsey. There were a few rare doubters who claimed he would fight himself to a standstill at the rate he was going, but theirs were faint cries in a thunderstorm of enthusiasm.

Every one but Archie had views on Archie. He let them all talk around him and said nothing. I don't think he knew what to say. I don't think he knew half of what the whole thing was about. He only knew that he had discovered swift magic in his limbs and was content for the promoter to do the rest. The promoter must have done quite a lot, for

Archie was on show at least once a week. People talked about his not being able to go on for ever, but when you are getting three pounds a time it seems to you that you can.

That was the way it struck Archie. He had no complaints. Nor had his family. Mrs. Griggs, who had been laundering and 'doing' doorsteps since the death of her husband a year before, now continued with only a part of it, as a 'hobby' — or to be more precise, for drink money. She was all for Archie's career. It was odd to recall her derision three months back at the idea of her 'little whipper-snapper' turning pugilist. Even after his conquest of the Novices' Cup that had given him hope of a professional career she still behaved the same way. There was a minor scene of a sort while he was telling us all about it at Joe's:

'Ah-a-rrchie!' She called him from her door up the street. She would never come near to do it. The point from where she first caught sight of him was considered good enough.

He gave her a petulant glance, but without stirring. He was enjoying himself.

She came shuffling up the street, swinging her arms from the elbow, like a belligerent sailor on leave. The rest of us gave her plenty of room.

'Called yer, didn't I?' she rasped, jutting out an underlip.

He said plaintively, still lolling on the window behind: 'Go '*ome*, Ma. I'll come soon. Gotta show me up, 'ave yer?'

'You come in this minute! Boxer . . . ! Box your ears, that's what I'll do!'

He hesitated for one more moment, then shambled off under her glare.

'Box some o' the Yids if he was more sensible!' she said to the world at large as she followed him.

With his rapid progress, especially on the financial front, she tyrannised him less — but other people more. She was very quarrelsome; a trifling difference with a neighbour would be enough to draw from her a threat to 'send me Archie after yer!' During the intervals of opening-time at

79

the pub she sat gossiping about Archie on the tenement steps in the next street. This was where the widows who did door-steps and washing waited to be hired. When the pub opened she would inveigle some of them from their livelihood for a drink and 'the latest news about my Archie'.

Her appearance remained unaltered through Archie's growing affluence. She would have probably considered buying clothes tantamount to throwing the money down the drain. Futile dolling yourself up at forty-five. In drink there was something age didn't spoil.

She never attended his fights. 'Saw enough scrapping with his father alive!' she told everybody, although Mr. Griggs had always seemed to us an essentially inoffensive man whose drinking, even, hinted at being an act of solidarity rather than an indulgence of self. She would spend the whole of Sunday afternoon toasting 'Archie's victory' in advance. It was Billy's job to bring her the decision immediately the show ended. Archie would by then have been taken off to the billiard hall by a jubilant Stinky. That she wasn't told. She was left to imagine him being lionised somewhere in the West End 'among the nobs'.

Archie too had changed very little. His new-found confidence merely found a sartorial outlet. He wore decent clothes for the first time. Actually, they were only decent in contrast to his former shabbiness. He had had them made by a Gentile tailor, in compliance with his mother's wishes; it was obvious that she carried her anti-Semitism to the point of personal inconvenience. The suit was of a peculiar mauve hue and very, very natty. You had the feeling that the tailor had originally intended it for a female garment and made some slight readjustments at the last moment to meet Archie's needs. Archie emphasised this effect by the incorporation of a graceful sway into his walk. He looked quite a number of things conspicuously unpugilist.

His first 'black eye' was an act of Providence. It was really purple in hue and matched the rest of him perfectly. He seemed much more an addict to cosmetics than the victim of an accident.

It was the penalty of new flights in ambition. He was fighting better men and over longer distances. His stamina didn't seem to be the same. Stinky suggested it was a question of 'getting used to the distance'. He forgot what he had once said about fighters overdoing things. Warnings never seem to come from friends but from those least personally interested and therefore also the least heeded. Nobody in Archie's immediate circle was troubled. In Archie himself there was probably an unconscious urge to ignore anything that could be construed as weakness. He simply could not afford to 'lay off'. His family had got used to depending on his fight money. He was no fifty pounds a fight performer, but a weekly wage-earner. He didn't dwell morbidly on the impossible. On the contrary: his elation reached its peak when his manager got him his first fifteen-rounder. He was a *top-liner*. It was an undoubted step up, though partly discounted by being staged at a minor hall whose proprietor could pay only little more than what Archie received for a ten-rounder at the Arena. But it was chiefly prestige that he was after here. Topping the bill even in a minor hall was no small feather in the cap.

There was some divided opinion on Archie's most important fight to date. Fifteen rounds for an adolescent was an engagement to think about twice. Archie was reminiscent of past 'boy wonders' who had unexpectedly fought themselves to a standstill — ex-pugilists at the age of fifteen. But nobody had the temerity to do more than whisper these things.

He travelled to the boxing-hall with a very thin band of supporters this time. As a mid-week engagement his bout was timed to start before most of us could have reached the place, besides making an expensive journey. We discussed him to the exclusion of all else on our perambulations that evening. We were sorry even if resigned to waiting until

next day for the result: he would return much too late and
tired for our questions.

We trailed home a little earlier, though, in the hope that
he had won some magically swift victory and was back
before us. Surprising the number of people who were out
at the doors, waiting. 'Even the old 'uns,' grinned Ginger.

We strolled up to a group of urchins clustered around the
lamp-post. There was a tension in the atmosphere that
reminded one of the Great War, when we had stood about
waiting for an air-raid.

'No result yet, eh?' said Ginger. The urchins were always
first to catch the whiff of any rumour.

They all stopped talking and gaped at us in a kind of
ludicrous surprise. Then one of them began talking rapidly,
as if to get in his word before the rest:

'Stopped the fight in the fifth! Ambulance took 'im. Mrs.
Griggs didn't half bash the copper when he came and told her
the noos! Be murders here t'night if they let her come back. . .'

'Coo!' said Ginger. What else was there to say?

Archie spent a month in the hospital and another three
in a convalescent home. That in itself proved he was suffering
from something more serious than a hiding. He had cracked
up from a hidden strain somewhere. His legs and heart were
later diagnosed as the trouble; not only was boxing now out
of the question for him, but strenuous action of any kind. A
miracle-maker was needed to find Archie 'light work'.

He spent his time leaning up at Joe's in the first weeks
home. He had a vacant and dispirited air about him, like
a chronic out-of-work. Maybe he was brooding on past
glories. He never talked 'fight' and nobody talked it to him.
Nobody talked to him much, anyway. Without the distinction of his boxing he was not a very interesting fellow.

The last tribute people paid him was the organising of a
collection to start him off in 'business'. Then they put him
out of their minds. They had their own troubles.

He was exactly sixteen when he took up his new career. The collection was enough to buy him a case full of men's underwear. Sympathisers in the market salvaged him a pitch between two barrows. Here he stood all day at the open case, like a cheap-jack about to draw a crowd. Only the cheap-jack's bluster was lacking; he hovered by the goods with a lost, helpless air, as if they had been planted on him by an unseen hand. Now and then he called out half-heartedly: 'What about some nice socks, gents?'

He became a regular fixture in the market. He looked like the other pedlars who had never known anything better. Only his queer mauve suit kept alive for people the memory of his past glory.

PART TWO

*

CHAPTER 13

The Sweat-shop

WHILE in a certain privileged section of the community this was the age that marked you as a 'growing boy', here in the East End you were a potential wife-keeper. Mothers of marriageable daughters were watchful for your first move, like a shopkeeper in ambush for window-gazers.

There was reason in their calculations. The clothing trade employing most of us was organised on such a system of long-established 'levels' that the level you attained as a youth made it possible to ascertain with a fair precision the level you would occupy as a man. At sixteen people knew whether you were likely to be a 'no-good', a 'steady fellow', or a 'bargain'. These followed each other in order of merit. Being labelled with the first pigeon-holed you as a fool or a crook who was at all costs to be avoided by ambitious virgins; the second a 'tryer' who was good enough for a girl without 'looks' or on the dangerous edge of spinsterhood; the third a go-getter who not only put work before all else but didn't *think* of anything else, a man well worth the dowry any girl could muster — for in his hands it would rather be an investment than an expense: that was the virtue valued above all others in a male. To be merely good-looking, healthy or clever in an unprofitable way didn't impress. You had to have the quality that 'got you somewhere'. If you had *that,* then you were just what mothers with marriageable daughters were looking for, irrespective of whether you were also, with it, deformed, defective, or dull.

You start work at a very low wage. It is supposed to be a concession to the boss for teaching you the trade. I began, I believe, with what must be the world's record in low wages. I got sixpence a week. The boss was a relative of a neighbour of ours and considered he was doing my people a special favour in having me in to work for him. Because of this I wasn't made to carry parcels to the shop. It was supposed to be 'degrading'; but he didn't think it correspondingly degrading to pay me sixpence a week in wages.

Mr. Begleiter was typical of sweat-shop bosses: a short, plump and fussy man continually urging others to 'put some life' into themselves. That was where his own exertions ended. He thought he himself personified the highest point in human evolution. He liked to remind me of it. 'It's by studying your work that you get there, my boy,' he was fond of saying. By getting there he meant becoming like him. He was a living portrait of the successful barbarian. In his thirty years' domicile he still could read no English except the back page of the *Star*, the dockets sent him by the shop and the names of all venereal diseases. He boasted of having once practised seventeen variations of the sexual act. Now his recreations were horse-betting, brandy-drinking and vapour baths. Once a year, on the Day of Atonement, he attended synagogue. And his favourite 'last word' in a discussion was: 'If you don't like what I say you can kiss my arse!'

Mr. Begleiter proceeded energetically to organise me. That is not to say he taught me the trade. He was too busy for that. He supervised my personal life instead. He gave me 'guidance'. I was a difficult boy: I had a peculiar habit of looking forward to the evening. In Mr. Begleiter's opinion this would be my ruin. 'Success' never came of watching the clock. When I reached for my jacket at eight p.m. Mr. Begleiter would ask how I intended passing the evening. He had a notion that outside the urgency of a wedding, a party, or a visit to a dying relative, an evening not spent in work was a frittering of time. He was very proud of having missed his own youth. It had helped to 'make him what he was'. And he wanted me to be the same. When I joined an athletic club later on and asked to leave a quarter of an hour earlier on the occasions I was to represent it in a boxing tournament, he was positively agitated on my behalf. He warned me not once but many times that sport 'wouldn't get me anywhere'. I'm afraid I was adamant. I could see his point. Sport could only give me health. I would never keep a wife and children on that.

Perhaps I was unusually unadaptable. I hadn't calculated on a sweat-shop in my childish plans. To be frank, I hadn't calculated on work at all at the time I was put to it. I imagined myself safe for at least another two years at the Central School I was attending. My parents had other plans. They felt that somebody in the family beside my father ought to do some work, and as I was the eldest of six children (my brother was by now married) they suddenly withdrew me from school a few weeks after I had turned fourteen. It was a long time before I forgave them that. It caught me totally unawares. There wasn't even a respite in which to accustom myself to the idea. I left on the last day of term, and on the first Monday of what should have been my summer holidays knocked at the door of Mr. Begleiter's workshop at eight o'clock of a very sunny morning.

Mr. Begleiter was still in his pants when he let me in. I followed him down the stairs and into the back-yard. Here we waded our way through various domestic utensils to the workshop. It was adjacent to the lavatory and you had presumably to know which was which by the smell.

I was the first arrival. Mr. Begleiter left me and returned to his breakfast. There was time for me to get acquainted with the new school in which I was to complete my education. It was a low room. Moving against the cluttered disorder of the fittings made me feel like a giant in a toy-shop.

Mice scuttled to and fro in a corner, in contemptuous indifference to my presence. There was an odour of stale perspiration. The floor was littered with bits of cloth, tattered newspapers and a very ancient, caked deposit left by a cat that was probably long dead.

The first weeks were naturally the hardest. All day you could hear the noise of the children playing in the street outside. It was like being imprisoned somewhere underground. The electric light had to be on all day on account of the poor daylight we got.

After the holidays it was a long time before I could learn to disregard the sound of the school-bell and the happy chatter of returning children. My old friends would stop on their way home to grimace playfully at me through the cellar-grating. Mr. Begleiter invariably chased them away. But each visit revived for me the memory of their freedom as contrasted to my own servitude and made the rest of the day a tormented, drawn-out penance.

The sweat-shop employee is unique among industrial workers in the possession of 'individualistic' illusions. As a piece-worker he is, to all appearances, his own master. He is entitled to demand as much as he can produce. This, naturally, does not make for punctuality in leaving, or a class coalition against the boss. 'He is one of us', is the feeling; and another feeling, less frequently articulated but as constant in every one's mind, is: 'Any one of us has the chance to be him.' It takes so little, after all. A bit of capital for fittings, a back room in the house partitioned off as 'workshop', and a wife and children to do the work. The more children the better. They have their uses in a sweat-shop worker's life.

The sweat-shop worker's prize seems always within snatching distance. A little extra industry will get it. There is proof of that in the mushroom growth of sweat-shops all over the district. The fact that these are abortive concerns mostly displacing identical ones that have flourished for only a season is something he turns a blind eye to. He prefers to look on the bright side of things.

Regular work is impossible. The whole trade is so controlled from the top that it is imperative to work all hours in the busy season in order to scrape through in the slack. The result is a paradox unparalleled in industrial life: six months of all work and no leisure, followed by six months of all leisure and no work. Or, translated in to more living terms: six months in which you have money to spend but no time in which to spend it, succeeded by six months in which you have plenty of time to spend money but no money to spend.

This system hits you with full force from the age of eighteen. Until then you are still a 'hand', that is a 'help' to a baster, presser, or machiner, and employed at a daily or weekly rate — putting you under no obligation to stay late. But there too punctuality will be considered as reflecting a casual attitude. You will be accused of having eyed the clock all day, and on reaching for your coat asked whether you have 'an important wedding on this evening?' The pressure increases tenfold when you are working 'on your own' later. As long as a machine is whirring you are expected not to budge from the bench. An obstinate punctuality will result in first deductions being made from *your* supplies when the slack comes. The boss will meet protests with the bland retort that it is his 'duty' to 'study first those who study me'.

Early in life you are confronted with the alternative of being a 'no-good' or a 'sweater'. As the first you will be one of those least able to hold down a job in the slack owing to what is termed your 'independence' in the busy; as the second you have a better chance of 'earning', but at the full cost of health and leisure. You must choose between being a wastrel and a slave. The middle alternative of functioning as a human does not exist.

CHAPTER 14

The Sweet Bloom of Womanhood

FOR a girl the situation was similar — but with qualifications. Like the young Jewish boy she too often passed from the school into the sweat-shop. In her case adaptation was, and still is to-day, much more of an ordeal. She has not consorted intimately with males before — and here at one step she is meeting them at their beastliest. In the past, males whom she has casually encountered 'talking dirt' have probably paused for her to pass out of earshot before resuming. They cannot do that now. She is with them to stay. They either have to treat her without an atom of respect or change the habits of a lifetime. It can be imagined which alternative they are likely to choose.

The metamorphosis the sweat-shop produces in the girl will be an even more thorough process than that produced in the boy. He as a street urchin was a quarter of the way there. For her the readjustment will involve greater conflict. But the result can hardly be different: she will in all probability turn out a hard-boiled, hard-bitten and occasionally hard-swearing young woman. She will have had several years' experience of sweat-shop ethics. If by that time she is not broken by it she is inured to it.

It is the subconscious fear of this prospect that is behind so many attempts to escape from the sweat-shop in the early stages. You will find a continual dribble to the large stores for employment as a 'sales lady' — the East End euphemism for shop-assistant. Here, in spite of the identical long hours of drudgery, the sweat-shop girl finds the complete antithesis of her other life. She is a 'lady'. People address her as 'Miss'

— not by her Christian name or some derisive nickname. Politeness is the watchword. To an ex-sweat-shop girl this is nothing short of a revolution.

Unfortunately — or so the workshop girls think — this branch of industry is as overcrowded as most. Employment in it also involves a high standard of 'presence'. Only the well-dressed and well-spoken are acceptable. For the sweat-shop girl an acquired elegance as well as an acquired elocution are things hardly come by.

What keeps so many in the sweat-shop, as well as what attracts them to it, is the relatively rapid promotion in pay. It is the opening which most obviously suggests itself to parents seeking to make use of a fourteen-year-old child. The real intricacies of the trade are not the girl's to master. The garment only comes to her in its last stages. Her job is to fasten down the lining and sew on the buttons. This takes no time to learn. She was probably familiar with work of this sort before ever entering a sweat-shop. All she has to acquire there is dexterity. She is already worth fifteen shillings to begin with, and her earnings rise with the growth of her turn-out.

She starts as help to an already established 'finishing hand' who is on piece-rates. Ultimately she too works 'on her own'. It only means a couple of years waiting — not five or six, like the boy.

In that time she will be gaining two kinds of experience: of work and of men. In both cases the older girl will be her example. Like her she will soon cease to flare up at language that is commonly supposed to make a 'good' woman leave the room. You can't afford to leave a room in which you earn your living. And one workshop is the same as another. You must learn to stifle your blushings. If you are the hardy sort you will eventually even get into the habit of recipro-cating the men's jests.

Nothing, however, will ever get you accepted by them as 'one of us'. They share a kind of solidarity that keeps you out. Their treatment of each other is definitely different from their separate treatment of a woman. You see this best illustrated in argument. The furthest they will go with each other is a crude truculence; with a woman they both begin and end with sexual insults. They will always receive preferential treatment from the boss in a wage-dispute: he 'explains the position' to them. But to the finishing hand who complains of the low price on a garment he will invariably retort: 'If it's not enough go and make up your earnings in Piccadilly!'

The pretty and plain girls have a hard time of it in rather different ways. Men do not blatantly insult the pretty girl. They prefer the finesse of the 'double-meaning' remark. A certain kind of man believes that tactics of this sort enhance his attraction in a woman's eyes. He never heeds a protest: he thinks it sheer coquetry. Usually it is the more repellent and frustrated of men who resort to this verbal form of masturbation.

For the plain girl there is not even this. She is an object of complete derision. They continually remind her of approaching spinsterhood. You feel they would give a lot to see it happen. She symbolises for them the plain wife their own loves have changed into. Sex has cheated them — ending as a repetition of their own parents' drudgery. And the only satisfaction is to revenge themselves on these plain — and usually husband-hunting — girls, whose every move they see as part of a diabolical plan to trap one more of their unfortunate sex.

Such circumstances have largely inspired the term 'workshop girl'. It is meant to be vaguely derogatory, like calling a girl a prostitute in a very mild way. Being a 'workshop girl' is considered to be not so much a way of earning a living as a way of living. It implies that you have seen sex at its ugliest. You are a kind of spiritually damaged goods. Your stock as a possible bride depreciates accordingly.

The change from schoolgirl to woman is a much more

rapid one than that of schoolboy to man. It is certainly more conspicuous. A boy is never quite a man while his face is smooth and his body thin. A girl has no troubles of this sort. She has only to put paint on her lips and high heels under her feet, and if she takes up her stand in Oxford Street a dozen men will approach her in as many minutes.

It takes one week's wages to make a woman out of a girl. This is what actually happens. The young finishing hand achieves it with her very first earnings. It is the price she exacts for her servitude.

Life from then on is one perpetual effort to belie reality. Her attire is cheaply and outrageously 'smart'. It is intended to allay any suspicions that she is a workshop girl. She is a film actress, a 'lady', anything you will — but not a workshop girl. Unfortunately the result reveals just what it is intended to conceal. 'Glamour' is not to be donned like a cloak. A thousand signs give her away.

She does her best to act as counterpart to the local male. She is actually an even more spurious and pathetic fake. A thousand restrictions hem her in. In other words, although she is allowed to dress up as her conception of a film actress, she is not allowed to behave as one. She is strictly controlled from home. True, she may parade the pavement: that 'shows her off'. But she cannot do it at all hours. A standard of respectability relatively equal to a nun's is imposed on her. The reason here is a more practical one. Virginity and a 'good name' are virtues very highly prized in Jewish life. Scandal of any sort brings down a girl's value in the marriage market. You will be surprised how insistent young men who are more familiar with venereal disease than most of us with the common cold are on 'purity' in a girl.

The marriage prospect is paramount. It is a girl's only hope of leaving the sweat-shop. She will end up, if necessary, by accepting literally anybody — if he provides an escape from the sweat-shop. It might turn out to be an 'escape' to a drudgery that many people would consider a lot worse.

But not the girl. For her there is no hell like the sweat-shop.

It is to marriage that she devotes all her young life's efforts. She is out to preserve two things until then: her 'good name' and her savings account. Together they form her dowry. The savings account is naturally the most important part; not because Jewish youths are out to blackmail parents for undertaking the job of keeping their daughters, but because of a parallel desire on their own part to escape the sweat-shop. This is only possible through the agency of a little capital to start something 'on one's own'.

The girl will marry at the earliest age permitted. She is a devout believer in the adage that 'opportunity only knocks at the door once'. Her main anxiety is to cash in on her looks while she has them; she knows the heavy and rapid toll they suffer from sweat-shop life. Age shows itself weekly. There is no such thing as a 'well-preserved woman' of thirty among sweat-shop females — let alone of forty, as among upper-class ones. The 'bloom' of a sweat-shop girl's life is about eighteen. If she has been lucky enough to preserve her freshness until then, she begins to lose it soon afterwards. At twenty-eight she can count herself pretty well finished as a marriage proposition. To young men she is a pathetic joke. I know of only two cases in my own experience of girls who married beyond that age; both of them had fairly substantial dowries to help matters and were married by widowers: that is, men whose youth and best passion departed from them in the company of their wives to the grave.

More than the usual amount of gossip surrounds such marriages. It goes on familiar lines:

'Wonder how she got herself a man so late?'

'Paid plenty, I suppose.'

'They say she has a tidy stocking saved. . . .'

'Y' might have thought it 'ud be about time she was making her will at her age!'

'S'pose he needed some one to look after the children.'

'Cheaper on the whole to have a wife than a house-keeper, they say.'

'Probably a case of 'ad to. . . .'

People deride the idea of 'love' in a late marriage. They look for ulterior motives. Unfortunately they are, in this class of society, mostly right: girls do not remain spinsters out of a sense of 'freedom' or in jealous preservation of a 'career'. Marriage can be the only possible career for them. Spinsterhood is a dismal admission of failure.

CHAPTER 15

That's how Tailors are Born

I STAYED at Mr. Begleiter's only ten weeks, owing to the fact that my wages rose by such minute increments that it was calculated I wouldn't reach a man's wage until I was due for an old age pension. I had been a better paying proposition to my parents at school. My father became energetic in a way that was characteristic when it was others and not himself who were in need of a job and soon found me another through an acquaintance of his. I left Mr. Begleiter at the end of one week and started at the beginning of the next at Mr. Feinstock's. Except that I got five shillings a week it wasn't very much of a change. Mr. Feinstock was also small, plump and bossy. I was convinced by that time that master-tailors were a special race of men created by a deity with a nasty sense of humour.

Mr. Feinstock's workshop was the real thing, not a converted bedroom. There were ten people at work there, counting his own two sons. It was oblong in shape, twenty feet by twelve, with whitewashed walls and a skylight so ancient that the heavens seen dimly through it were perpetually dismal, even in June weather.

The fittings were few, but none the less crowded for that. Down one wall were ranged the three basters' benches, down the other six treadle machines, of which only four were in use. The other two were being kept for an 'emergency rush', for which, as far as I know, Mr. Feinstock is still waiting. Across the narrow far wall of the workshop were the presser's bench and the finishing-hand's small table and stool. The middle was reserved exclusively for the dummies and as a gangway down which Mr. Feinstock could stride in his agitated moments.

Eight a.m. was the official hour for work to begin. Some of the men came earlier in the height of the rush, but nobody had ever beat Mr. Feinstock to it. He was always there when you arrived. There was, in fact, no definite evidence that he left the place at night.

He was a great stickler for punctuality in the morning. If you walked in at ten-past eight he asked whether you had 'enjoyed your morning off'. But his meticulousness strangely deserted him in the evening. As you reached for your jacket at eight o'clock he would look up with an air of great surprise and say, clicking his tongue fretfully: 'Well, well, eight o'clock already. Who would believe it — with so little done?' Mr. Feinstock's idea of a day's work was for you to get rid of his entire season's stock by evening.

He spent most time in the cutting-room upstairs in the house. Here he got the work ready for the men, interviewed callers and had violent squabbles with his wife. You could never be certain which of these he was doing. They were all performed with an equal degree of noisiness.

It was his eldest son, Moe, who was in charge down at the workshop. He was twenty-two, small like his father, but, unlike him, thin. He tried to imitate his fussiness, but it had an unreal air about it, like the bloodless motions of a clock-work figure. His features were small and pointed and he perpetually wore a fretful look so that it would make people ask him why he looked worried and he could reply, 'About business.' He never called the workshop 'the workshop'. It was always 'the business'.

Moe was very self-conscious about his 'responsibility'. He rarely joined in general laughter, thinking it childish. In dealing with Mr. Feinstock he addressed him not as 'Daddy', like his brother, but rather gravely as 'Father'.

He worked as baster at one of the benches. In between he was supposed to manage everybody else, including me.

96

But he only became aware of my existence when he wanted a bet taken out to the bookie at the corner. I was very reluctant about going. I didn't show it at first, through fear of derision. You weren't thought much of if you didn't bet, drink, smoke, and like 'tarts'. These were regarded as the universal practices, except among priests.

Secretly I hated bookies and their like. It wasn't their ethics that antagonised me — but their looks. Had they been quiet, diffident sort of fellows who accepted the slip from you with a deprecatory smile and some whimsical quip or other about the ways of human nature I should probably have thought them charming and been a confirmed punter to this day. Alas, bookies do not study the wants of my sort of client. I was lost to them from the beginning. And I resented Moe's efforts to change me; on about the sixth or seventh occasion I refused to go. He stared at me in absolute astonishment. He couldn't make me out at all.

'What's up?' he said. Some of the others had stopped work in their amazement and were listening.

'Must be religious,' said one.

I shook my head confusedly but quite determinedly. 'Don't wanna go to the bookie,' was all they could get out of me.

The thing naturally put my stock down, but to my way of thinking it was the lesser evil of the two. Later Moe made one more half-hearted try to lure me for these errands, which I again frustrated, and after a word from my father to his father let me alone. My mother was rather proud of my 'stand'. She didn't know of my peculiar private aversions. She thought I was the kind of boy who resisted 'temptation'. It is a pity that I had to destroy this illusion for her later on.

Mr. Feinstock's other son, Judah, who was eighteen, was quite unlike Moe. He was a placid sort. All day he sat happily humming the 'latest numbers' to the accompaniment of his busy fingers. Musical shows were his one pleasure. These were what he laboured for. Every Sunday morning he would arrive humming a number from the new show he had seen the night before. A show didn't have the same interest for him after a long run. He was only keen about it in its first week, for then he could hum songs that nobody else knew.

He was an easy-going youth and very obliging. When he came in to work he had a cheery, high-pitched 'Good morning' for everybody. The only quarrels he had were with his father. Mr. Feinstock was continually subtracting sums from his wages on the vague grounds of 'not having had such a wonderful week this week'. With somebody working on piece-rates this was a particularly insolent encroachment. Judah resented it fiercely. When the books were made up every Thursday and each worker called in turn to the cutting-room to confirm the week's output Judah ended his own interview with Mr. Feinstock by rushing down into the workshop for his jacket, bitterly denouncing the system of 'working for your own father'. This scene occurred with tedious regularity. Judah was perpetually in the position of 'leaving at the end of the week'. But always at the last moment some hurried consultations took place behind the family walls and when you came in to work on Sunday morning there was Judah at his bench happily humming the 'new number' he had picked up the night before.

He was his mother's acknowledged favourite. I believe it was she who played a large part in getting him returned the subtracted part of his wages each week. She was full of him — his 'lovely tenor voice', his 'beauty', his 'cleverness'. 'Mine Judah', she called him, and when he talked she looked at him proudly, as if it was a trick that nobody else could do.

She came to call 'the boys' and Mr. Feinstock upstairs for tea every morning at nine-thirty and she wouldn't budge until Judah had accompanied her. For the others she considered she had done her duty in calling them. She was a large, slow, creaking sort of woman. What I remember most was her untidiness. You never saw her in anything but a thin and hastily donned linen dress: it was as though she performed her household tasks in between long shifts of sleep. When she came shuffling into the workshop in the morning you had the impression that she had with great difficulty only just extricated herself from a haystack. There she stood at the entrance, waiting for Judah to leave, her feet astride, one hand on a vast hip, the other scratching thoughtfully at her hair. If she had to wait long she made some light conversation about her 'complaints': these were certain unspecified aches that nobody had the temerity to investigate further. She would finish by shuffling out into the yard with a suddenly acquired limp or cough to give the whole business authenticity.

In the summer she liked to sit in the back-yard. A table was put there for her to prepare the family's meals. It was supposed to be a cheap way of getting 'fresh air' at work. She had a sister-in-law who dropped in for long visits and incurred the men's everlasting enmity by invariably propping herself up in a chair against the lavatory door and making it considerably embarrassing for any one to enter. They labelled her 'The Guardian Angel'.

In the busy they were joined by Rachel, the finishing-hand. Letting her work 'in the open' was, Mr. Feinstock pretended, a special privilege. Actually it was a matter of his own convenience, for his wife gave some help on those occasions and it made the work easier for them if they sat together.

Rachel had worked several years for Mr. Feinstock. That was why he pinched her bottom in passing and spoke to her in language only equalled by that he used to his wife. She was, as he often put it, 'like my own daughter'; and he accordingly proceeded to treat her as some people do treat their daughters. As a result, regular crises were precipitated in which Rachel, like Judah, was on the verge of 'leaving'. Sometimes it was of her own accord, sometimes she was dismissed. But whichever it was she was there working as usual on the following week.

She was a girl of twenty-seven, with a meagre, pimply face and bony shoulders. Her nose was thin, long, and despondent and buried deep in her work. At Mr. Feinstock's abuse she grew very upset and stitched away fretfully. When she could endure him no longer she cried in a plaintive and harassed voice on the edge of tears: 'I've had enough of this. You can get a different girl in to insult!' And she continued stitching away even more fretfully than before.

I usually left too early to see the sequel. Next morning, however, I would notice a sort of exaggerated unobtrusiveness about Mr. Feinstock's movements. He would go around giving people instructions in a low, intimate voice, like a sister in a hospital ward. Rachel was the privileged patient. He didn't, as before, throw her coats for finishing from wherever he happened to be standing. He would bring them personally, lay them gently across her bench and whisper in the kind of syrupy voice calculated to induce a patient to swallow a nasty pill: 'See to this coat, if y' don't mind, Rachel.' For Mr. Feinstock this was almost old-world gallantry.

By the afternoon he would have got over this strange affliction and a certain brusque note have crept into his directions. By tea-time he would be his old, familiar, insulting self once again and you could conjecture, with a certain amount of precision, the moment at which their next quarrel was due.

Mr. Feinstock had two separate opinions of Rachel, each of which he reserved for the appropriate moment. When she worked overtime she was a 'good girl' with a heart of 'pure gold'. He wouldn't wish for a better wife for his sons. If he himself had been younger and unmarried — he raised a pair of significant and challenging eyebrows at the workshop: 'Think I don't mean it?' the grimace implied.

His displeasure with her invariably coincided with a lapse in memory: he completely forgot about her 'heart'. He suddenly discovered certain 'habits'. He recorded aloud the number of times she stopped work to dab at her face in a pocket-mirror. He seemed to keep a private time-table of her movements.

Everybody else gladly took up the cue to relieve their boredom. You could have endless 'fun' with her about her 'looks': she was continually trying out new styles of hairdressing, in the vain hope of stumbling across something startlingly appropriate. The men became exaggeratedly interested in her. Each time she appeared newly coiffured they competed in guessing the identity of the film actress she was allegedly imitating.

She was very popular between nine-thirty and ten in the mornings. That was when she brought the tea from the kitchen. It was 'Good old Rachel' from all sides and she flushed with a timid pleasure. She probably looked forward to that moment even more than they.

I used to spend a lot of time on a low stool at her bench, pulling out the bastings of the finished coats. She talked what was for her quite intimately to me, for I was a boy and didn't regard her with a man's cynical eyes. She would say facetiously: 'When are you going to take me out?' — and laugh with a kind of coy pleasure at my embarrassment.

Mostly she told me her troubles. Her mother and younger sisters were perpetually nagging at her to find a husband. 'It's not so easy,' she said plaintively. 'You don't know who to trust among the men these days.' She liked to think it was her discriminating taste that kept her single.

She was also worried about her looks. She would be frequently asking me in an anxious whisper 'what age I would take her for'. I always said twenty-two. Once, when she seemed particularly on the *qui vive* for my answer, I said *nineteen* and she muttered with downcast eyes: 'You're making fun of me, like the others.' I hastily defended myself, saying, 'You can't really tell a girl's age, you know.' This reply seemed to please her very much, although to this day I don't know what I meant by it.

Sometimes she fished a pair of spectacles out of her bag and put them on surreptitiously. She would stare at me to see whether I was laughing. 'I never wear them outside,' she would explain several times over. She thought spectacles destroyed sex-appeal and was very anxious to make it clear that she didn't habitually wear them.

She told me about her 'love affairs'. She used this term to describe anything from two words with a man to a nudge in the ribs. She harped a great deal on her respectability. Some women would let a man do anything. She inferred that she could have been married a dozen times over had she been that sort. She was 'particular'. No man would be allowed to go too far with her. She preferred to wait for the 'right one'. This legendary hero turned up unfailingly in the pages of *Woman's Weekly* and she had no doubt her own turn for a visit would come one day.

Her 'real trouble' was that she had excruciatingly 'bad luck'. There were her sisters, for instance. They were much better-looking than she. She was afraid to take a man into the house in case of a sudden switch-over in his affections. Her name also put her at a disadvantage: who could fall in love with a girl called Rachel? 'I'm *Ray*, outside,' she confided in me. She felt it was the best she could do in the circumstances, but that it still fell short of satisfactory. She thought a name like Monica or Madeleine would have changed her entire history.

She was sad when I had to leave a year later, in one of the slack seasons. She had a notion that I was the only one who had 'understood' her. 'Are you going to take me out when you grow up?' she asked facetiously.

'Of course,' I said uncomfortably. 'But you'll probably

be married by then.'

'Yes,' she said. 'Maybe.' She didn't seem very confident about it.

'Anyway,' she added in a kind of sorrowful anger, 'you'll probably turn out like the rest of them. They're all alike in this trade!'

I had a vague premonition she would be right.

CHAPTER 16

Killing Time

YOU don't feel unemployment so badly in the first days. A late and leisurely breakfast helps you to see things in a philosophical light and the sight of other lads 'in the same boat' when you step into the street tends to strengthen that view. They are chatting around Joe's as if it was evening. There is no sense in 'hands' looking for work in the slack. They are a special class of conscripts called up in the busy. It seems a crazy system to you at that age, but you go out to make the best of it.

At Joe's you glance through the papers and see what the world is up to. The world seems to be up to quite a lot. You realise for the first time that more things than you imagined happen outside the workshop. You didn't know it before. There is no time to read newspapers in the busy season.

The day's programme depends on your financial status. If you are over sixteen years of age it might be signing-on day for you at the Exchange, and off you go. If you are under sixteen you will have to make some sort of attempt to seek work. There is supposed to be more chance for a very young apprentice. In any case you have to show your people you are doing something about it, even though your efforts come to nothing. Parents like to feel that you have exhausted every possible channel.

So a few of us would set off on the tramp. We studied the bills in the trimming-shop windows closely, but welcomed any diversion of duty. When we met anybody we knew we stopped for a chat. If a couple of girls came our way we tried that too. It was nice to feel you could now do in the daytime what you had always had to wait for the evening to do.

We rollicked along the street like sailors on leave. Sometimes we sang songs in chorus. We stopped to watch any trivial 'sight' along the way, even if it was only men digging up the road. We made grimaces through the windows to girls in the department stores. The street seemed a much more interesting place than the workshop.

That was how things were the first days. Saturday gave you a jolt. You realised you were stale and restive. You recalled the old feeling of exhilaration at the end of a week in the workshop. There was nothing now to make you feel it was the week-end. You couldn't even change into another suit of clothes. If you were so lucky as to possess a 'new' suit you would have been wearing it during the week and it didn't make a change putting it on on Saturday.

The week-end seems longer than the other five days put together. You hang around watching people who are in work go off to a dance or to the pictures. For the rest of us it has to be Joe's once again, or a tramp down to the West End to look at the places we can't afford to enter.

Your 'freshness' is a mere memory with the opening of the second week. You begin to hate the sight of the streets. You know the programme before you start. You get up later in the mornings if you can. You are now desperately out to kill time.

I think it was worse for us under-sixteens. It was not only the money we missed. We were afraid we might be long enough out of work to forget the little we had learned.

Meanwhile we tried getting temporary jobs in other trades. If there was a notice outside a warehouse advertising for 'A Strong Boy', you went inside to apply; but there were invariably a dozen or more 'stronger' boys than yourself queued up in there already.

We tried jumping on the back of carts in the afternoon

for a ride. But the long trek back was depressing. It may have killed time, but it also nearly killed you into the bargain.

It gives an excuse to sleep late next morning. But time has its revenge on you for these inconsistencies: you find yourself very much alive at bed-time. You hang around Joe's for as long as there is other company, but eventually you have to turn in — probably to face a night of insomnia.

When you get resigned to unemployment as a chronic fact you try and take the edge off the week by going to a film matinée on Monday. You find the 'Splendide' very nearly full a half-hour before the show is due. It was a local adage that 'if you killed Monday you somehow get through the rest of the week'.

Inside the cinema you couldn't doubt the existence of this murderous intention. People were definitely out to get an afternoon's entertainment — in the most diabolical sense of the word. In the half-hour preceding the show they turned the place into a circus. They stood up and shouted jests to each other. Some sought out relatives and friends and when they had caught sight of them screeched across: 'Hey, Becky! Here's a seat I've saved for you — come on over!'

With the commencement of the programme the noise does not so much quieten down as change its character. It takes a more collective form. People accompany the theme-tune in a talkie with a whistle. They make facetious comments at the crucial moments in a drama. And underlying these intermittent noises the incessant crackling of pea-nuts and the squelch of sucked oranges makes a theme-tune of its own.

There are also the 'commentators' everywhere. These are usually housewives, for Monday is 'forgetfulness day' for them as well as for the unemployed. They love discussing the film during its progress. Mostly it is a drama that sets them off — they try predicting the various situations before they arrive. They do it with a great sense of triumph. They consider themselves very clever, like people who work out a crossword puzzle.

They were unbearable during an interesting film. Yet shifting from them might only be an exchange for a seat adjoining a peanut crackler or orange squelcher. There was one effective method a friend of mine only discovered several years later; it came from his habit of smoking a cheap brand of tobacco that was popularly suspected of having equine origins. It occurred to him to put its unpopularity to use. He set it smoking on one occasion, clenching his pipe in the corner of his mouth with the bowl facing the row behind. You wouldn't believe the speed with which those chattering women behind were sent spluttering into silence. More than that: his efforts completely cleared the row within five minutes. It was cruel, but it had to be done. We had a dismal week facing us and we couldn't afford to throw away our Monday afternoon.

Later we learned the trick of whiling away an afternoon at the Public Baths. I wish I could claim it was cleanliness alone that prompted the move; unfortunately the time-killing motive entered here too. It may not have been as absorbing a pastime as the cinema, but like the cinema it was a change from the streets.

The inducement here was the cheaper week-day prices and the permission to occupy a cubicle indefinitely. It was a refreshing change from the usual Friday night invasion of toil-weary hordes. Week-day custom was sporadic and confined mainly to three types of patron: unemployed youngsters, old Jews and turbaned Indian pedlars. The youngsters were least businesslike in intention. Washing was a consideration secondary to that of 'having a good time': this comprised unsolicited solos from various unmusical people and sporadic outbreaks of community singing. A catchy tune started by one invariably infected the rest. You never ultimately learned with whom you had been singing, but that didn't worry you. A kind of camaraderie enveloped us all and you might have thought we were tired businessmen relaxing like children, instead of unemployed youths secretly dreading the afternoon's end.

The old Jews proclaimed their presence with their frequent plaints for attendance. You always knew the occupant of a cubicle from which you heard a guttural call for: 'More hot water for No. 4, Guv'nor!' 'Guv'nor' is the old Jew's form of address for all persons in authority, from a bath-attendant to a Labour Exchange supervisor.

Most mystifying were the pedlars. You never heard them. They were seemingly engaged in the all-absorbing task of getting rid of dirt. You saw them enter the bath as uncompromisingly dark Asiatics, but if you happened to be about when one of them was leaving, he struck you as having much more of an affinity with the yellow races.

You got into a kind of unemployed rut — equivalent, but without the advantages, to the rut you had previously got into as a worker: you were always doing the same things. Also the things you could do annually narrowed down in scope. At seventeen you couldn't get a kick out of taking a ride on the back of a cart. You had outlived the pleasures of the fifteen-year-old. True that you might be getting something from the dole, but it wasn't much if your hobbies were smoking and taking out girls.

You became ashamed of looking pleasure-goers in the face at the week-end. A friend and myself tried to get jobs that would give us something for the week-end, if nothing else. We applied for casual work at the docks. This is a dangerous thing for Jews to do: it is regarded by the Gentiles as gate-crashing an occupation traditionally their own. Fortunately we didn't particularly look or speak like Jews.

It was really appearance that mattered most. With caps pulled over our eyes and 'chokers' wound round our throats we looked as if we could push a truck with the best of them.

Killing Time

We were picked out of a clamouring crowd by the foreman on our very first morning. We trooped into the wharf with the rest of the lucky ones to clock on. Then we were shown where to get our trucks.

At one minute to eight we stood in a circle under the head foreman's eyes. In the dimly-lit shed it looked as if we were assembled for an enlarged séance. The foreman had a whistle ready. I knew we would have to do something when he blew it, but I hadn't the faintest idea what. I was sure it couldn't be a truck-race to the opposite wall and back. I asked an old-timer beside me, 'Where do we go, mate?' He stared at me hard, then turned away disdainfully. He didn't like jokes that time of morning. A more friendly fellow on the other side who had overheard, volunteered: 'Down to the ole dock there, son.' I followed his glance. At the far end of the shed, a hundred yards away, was a wide doorway through which you could see the stevedores getting the cranes of the ship in working order. I spat on my hands, as the other men were doing.

'Ready?' called the foreman. We gripped the cold wooden handles of our trucks.

'Peeeeep!' We were off.

For a whole morning we wheeled our trucks to and fro across the bumpy ground. The goods were orange-crates. You had to take each delivery unloaded on you at the ship's side to its appropriate storeroom. Everybody except us seemed to know where to go. We were continually asking people the way. We began to be afraid we would become conspicuous in our wanderings. A foreman sitting on an upturned box near a goods-escalator seemed to be watching us. 'Let's ask him the way?' my friend suggested. It would show him we weren't loafing.

We wheeled our trucks towards him. He was about thirty yards distant. He wore a bowler hat and you couldn't see his expression very clearly, for his face was half-buried in the large upturned collar of his overcoat.

'Where do we take this?' my friend called out as we drew near.

There was no movement from the foreman.

'Where do we take this, please?' my friend repeated in a slightly louder voice.

The foreman still didn't stir, but slowly opened one baleful eye, like a cat disturbed from slumber. We began to move off with our trucks.

'You shouldn't have woken him up like that,' I said.

We were 'put off' at the end of the morning. It also happened to most of the other casuals. You never knew how long you were hired for when you were signed on. It might be a half-day, it might be a few days. There were no guarantees. It was your business to be waiting outside the wharf at seven-thirty each morning on the off-chance of work. Each day you had to re-win your job.

We were there times without number, but were successful in very small proportion to our efforts. Sometimes there was nothing for weeks. It was humiliating to leave the house at seven-fifteen each morning and return at eight-fifteen with one's lunch all intact. It frayed parental nerves as well as one's own. Nobody can consistently stand getting all worked up for nothing.

CHAPTER 17

Oh, to be in England

ONE particular period in the year was anathema to all, alike to those in work as to those out of it. This was the summer. It descended like a scourge, as the rainy season does in the tropics, making the normal continuance of life impossible. We saw no poetry in sunshine. It was just another burden from nature to add to those already imposed on us by man.

Personally I have no knowledge of those legendary happy faces of which the new sun is reputed to be the harbinger. I have no knowledge of them, that is, outside romantic novelettes. The kind of faces I associate with the sun's arrival are gloomy, furrowed ones. Its light did not flatter our neighbourhood. There is nothing more pathetically sordid than mean streets exposed in all their ugliness by the sun.

The main problem was not to get in the way of the sun's rays but to dodge them. People continually moved their chairs to whichever side of the street got the shade. They hated the sun. They talked about it in the same opprobrious terms they used for the rain and snow. When they said, 'Wonder how long *this* is going to last?' it wasn't exultation that you detected in their tone, but gloom. Summer was one long service of prayer for winter.

In the workshop there was escape from the sun's rays, but not from their effect. The men would strip to the waist, like coal-miners. Until a late age my own brazenness stopped short at a vest.

The only other device for relief was to open wide the

single small window usually provided in workshops, but as this unfailingly looked out on the back-yard, it is doubtful whether the current coming from that quarter was an improvement.

Work itself continued apace. Delivery was as urgent a matter for the manufacturer in summer as in winter. Often we were working in electric light, switched on to augment the sun's last fading rays.

I got up extra early. The freshness of the streets at seven-thirty was practically the only freshness you were likely to taste in the day's twenty-four hours and it was best to make the most of it. I meandered through back-turnings for as long as I could. I came as near to the fear of leaving them for the workshop as I had feared leaving the light for the dark in childhood.

I eventually reached the workshop in a mood of murderous resignation. Most people shared it with me, particularly on Monday mornings; our presser, a taciturn, toil-weary warrior with an occasional sardonic wit, would greet us regularly with the words: 'Only five more days to the week-end, boys!'

Unemployment proved itself no solution, either. It might have served some purpose had our neighbourhood been a rural one. The way things stood, however, it is problematical whether being exposed to the sun's glare in dusty streets was preferable to being 'protected' from it in an evil-smelling workshop. In both there was the same compulsion to be on one's feet all day — though not, in the one case, doing a job of work, but in looking for it.

Occasionally desperation changed the direction of one's feet from the Exchange to that of the park. This was two and a quarter miles distant, the nearest thing we had to a large open-air space. There you could find release from care beneath a tree, or in the sun itself (though here a clean and fresh sun), and from which you could return rested and tanned — to boast at the street corner later of the glorious time you had had 'at Southend where both the weather and the girls had been tip-top. . . .'

Our neighbourhood had the appearance of a large, untidy camp. People sat outside their doors from one dawn to the next. You had to walk in the gutter to avoid treading on them on your way home from anywhere.

Most domestic violence, I can recall, broke out this time of year. People's feelings were in a constant state of irritation. Most of the illegitimate babies, I should imagine, also had their origin in nights spent on the paving-stones of Shovel Alley or on the landings of the neighbouring tenements.

Nocturnal life in the tenements in summer was the rowdiest — on account, people said, of it being bug-ridden. Whether it was actually more so than most houses it is hard to tell. The occupants themselves were, in the way of working people, reticent about this aspect of their poverty. I don't know why. God knows bug-ridden homes are more to the shame of a landlord than his tenants!

Ever since I have known them, however, the tenements have suffered exclusively under this gibe. Probably it arose from the habit of its occupants to gossip at their doors long after the hour of summer bed-time; this might have signified ultra-sociable leanings on their part, but people, as they always do, preferred a nasty explanation.

I can only speak with authority of my own home. We had six rooms, but they were so tiny that the house was rather like a tall box-room partitioned off into six sections. Privacy had only a technical existence. It was like sleeping in separate bunks rather than rooms, except that we couldn't see each other.

The house was not yet in that stage of dilapidation that induces bugs to make it their permanent home. They came in the hottest periods only, like swallows to the Riviera. Sleep was then abandoned even by the most optimistic. Led by my mother we turned out *en masse* to engage the Enemy in single-handed battle. Paraffin was our heavy artillery, but this was employed only as a last resort, for the smell of it in the stifling heat turned the youngest of us sick and made even the hardier ones blench. We would usually have to fall back on it all the same — which would lead to a stampede not only of the invaders but of the defenders.

In our beds once again we would lean our heads on a cushion spread out on the window-sill and in that position try to snatch some sort of a doze, for the evil combination of paraffin and heat made breathing in the room itself impossible. Waking in the morning would be like trying to fight off the effect of a drug.

The most restive of us all was my father. Though ordinarily a sound sleeper, the heat put him completely out of joint, perhaps because of his stoutness. *His* excursions to the water-tap at night were the most frequent. On one occasion he announced his intention of making his bed in the back-yard; he disliked the marauding cats far less than the heat.

It wasn't they who ultimately terminated his sleep, but a violent and unexpected thunderstorm which drenched him before he was half-awake and drove him into the house to spend the rest of the night drying himself.

CHAPTER 18

A Youthful Idyll

'LOVE' first happened to me at the new club I joined during my third job. This club was much on the style of the previous one; I joined it because I discovered that the form of athletics I favoured was supervised by a rather more capable instructor. I only attended a couple of evenings a week for an hour or so and hurried round to Joe's afterwards.

I soon found that there was a girls' section also. It wasn't on the same premises, but safely ensconced in a different building a couple of streets away. I rarely saw it even then. There were 'socials' organised there every fortnight or so in the winter and after attending one I could understand why the place was referred to among the boys as the 'Old Maids' Society'. They were the dowdiest collection of girls possible. They tittered instead of talked, they let themselves be walked down the street in crocodile file like schoolgirls and they perpetually wore black stockings. Admittedly half the onus was on the club officials: upper-class busybodies who had come down East to teach these girls 'the better life'. It never occurred to them to do it by giving them good food and homes. They thought that if they turned them into neuters the other troubles would solve themselves. But perhaps some blame should also be attached to the girls for submitting to a tyranny and then making of it a virtue.

I became friendly with Minka Salomen because she was 'different'. That, I believe, is the reason most young men claim for falling in love. Nobody likes to admit having fallen in love merely because it is natural to do so.

Minka seemed 'different' because she didn't droop like the rest. She was very forthright and confident in her behaviour. It was not a very conspicuous quality in that club. She was a High School girl and that also, I dare say, appealed to me. I was very susceptible to people with 'nice' ways. I hadn't yet forgiven my parents for abruptly taking me from school and robbing me, as I thought, of a possible future among the monopolisers of 'nice' ways.

Minka was only fifteen and a half, but rather well-built and supple. She belonged to that category of schoolgirls who 'develop' rather quickly and are more sophisticated at thirteen than their mothers are at thirty. It attracted me perhaps because I was inarticulate myself. We made friends at the second club 'social' I attended. Actually it was she who did the making: she took possession of me while the rest of the respective sexes were eyeing each other furtively from opposite walls. I am sure mere chance made her choose me to 'start the ball rolling'. Perhaps I looked the shyest of the boys. Once she had me she kept me for the rest of the evening. I was an attentive listener. There was no alternative role for me; she was a tremendous talker. I was rather glad than otherwise. Had the prospects of conversation rested on me the outlook would have been bleak.

I can't for the life of me remember a word she said. It was all on minor club matters. She flitted from subject to subject like a society hostess dispensing small talk. It wasn't meant to be replied to. She thought I was interested because I stared at her all the time she spoke. I did it because I liked watching her face. I had never had a close-up of a girl's face for so long before. At a quick glance you might have thought her plain, but the longer you watched the more you found in her. She had dark eyes with dancing lights in them. They imparted an individuality to her face.

We walked home together after I had asked her permission. I had the feeling that if I hadn't done so after her sacrifice of a whole evening to me I could never have looked her in the face again.

She lived almost on the verge of the dock district. As we passed through streets whose character showed less and less trace of 'Jewishness' I had a wary eye about me. They were always a bit more rough with 'couples' in the Gentile quarter. I wondered what had made her come here. All the way through the long winding street in which she lived we didn't pass one Jew. For that matter we didn't pass many English. It was a quarter given over to Lascars, Malays and the hotch-potch of foreign ports. I recognised the place as one we had been warned to keep away from as children. Urchins of an indefinable shade of skin played in the gutters and strange men with scarred faces lumbered by in the dark. I was shocked at the idea of her living here. Many of the houses were supposed to be brothels, or lodging-houses for the coloured seamen — one didn't make a distinction between the two those days.

I was glad when she began to slow down about half-way through. This was supposed to be the tamer part. Things got worse as you neared the docks. Her house was just after a baker's, and before a cinema: she seemed in fairly respectable company.

We stopped before the shuttered window of the ground floor. She pointed a finger upwards. 'Third floor — that's mine.' I thought she must have pretty broad-minded parents. Most girls weren't allowed to take a boy farther than the street-corner before they were seventeen.

We leaned against the window-sill. It was a fairly well-lit spot, because of the cinema next door being open. There were some youths rollicking near its entrance and I had one eye on them all the time we talked. I was wondering whether the evening would pass without incident. I had to decide what line I would take if the youths began paying us attention. There were about half a dozen of them and I was sizing them up. I sought out the toughest. I knew from experience that *he* would be the problem — not their numbers. If you successfully bash the toughest, the others just vanish into the night.

After a five-minute furtive scrutiny I came to the conclusion that I might possibly handle the toughest one — unless there was some hulking brute of a pal lurking round the corner. The thought made me despondent again.

'Why do you look so sad?'

'Me?' I hadn't realised she had stopped talking. I had been full of the knotty problem in chivalry those youths had set me.

'It's the poor light makes me look like that,' I said.

'If it's them you're worrying about' — she jerked a thumb sideways at the youths — 'don't! They never worry me.'

'No?' I said hopefully.

'It only takes a word from my mother to send them running.'

'Really?' I felt myself growing enthusiastic about her mother.

'She must be a tough sort,' I said.

'You bet. Look for yourself!'

I peered beyond her. On the doorstep a yard away a little woman was perched. She nodded readily at me, as if she had been waiting all the time for my acknowledgement. Only her eyes were clear to me in the dimness. They had twinkling lights and creased to mischievous slits when she smiled, like Minka's.

'Cute, isn't she?' said Minka. 'She's all I've got. My father died of tuberculosis in the War.'

'Have you ——?' I stopped myself in time. I had nearly asked whether she had inherited his complaint, for she had a hoarse, throaty cough that broke out at intervals.

'Minka!' Her mother called to her in just the tinkling voice you would have expected to come from such a little woman. 'Come on, Minka. Time for bed.' I peered round at her in curiosity and she smiled again, as if to reassure me of her goodwill.

'Righto, Mother,' Minka responded almost at once. 'Well,' turning to me, 'I dare say we'll meet again at the club?'

I nodded.

'Good night.'

'Good night. Good night.' I gave them each a separate greeting and moved off. Half-way down the street I heard their door close. I retraced my footsteps and crossed the road to look up at their window. Above the lace curtain in the lower half the ceiling was bathed in a greenish-yellow gas-light. It made me feel melancholy to look at it, but I remained there a long time.

I really hoped to see her again before the fortnightly 'social', but did nothing about it. It was a bit of luck for me when I heard of the table-tennis tournament being held between the boys' and girls' clubs. I was amongst the audience that fateful evening. I kept my eyes steadfastly on the games, but I knew after five minutes that she wasn't present. You would have been bound to hear her laughing somewhere. She had a laugh that was a sort of natural consequence of her dancing eyes; I would have recognised it anywhere. I felt rather more downhearted than I'd expected to be. Perhaps she'd turn up later? Actually I had little hope of it.

A girl sidled up to me. 'Minka's not well to-day,' she said casually.

I felt myself go red and my first instinct was to stare through the girl. However, I merely felt myself go redder and redder and finally mumbled, 'Isn't she?'

'The usual thing,' she sighed.

I nodded. I had begun to get an idea what that meant.

'Why not go and see her?'

I muttered some kind of confused assent, but stood my ground. I didn't intend to walk off obediently at her orders.

I slipped out a quarter of an hour later. I felt I ought to get her something, but there was nothing open except the fried-fish shops. I entered her street warily and went the more warily the farther I penetrated it.

I stopped at her door. It was open, and some children were playing on the step. They looked at me curiously. 'Oojer want, mister?' said a little boy. 'Ma ain't come 'ome from the pub yet if it's 'er.'

I shook my head and let the knocker drop once.

'You gotta knock free times for the Jews,' said a little girl.

I nodded, uncomfortably. Just then a woman came shuffling out of the interminable darkness of the passage.

'Oojer want, son?'

'Name of Salomen.'

'Oaw.' She shuffled back, and I heard her bellowing up: 'Mrs. Salomen . . . !' A door opened somewhere above. 'Here's Minka's fella come, Mrs. Salomen!' She took no notice of my denials: 'Straight up — third floor. She's down again with trouble, poor bitch!'

I went slowly up three short, winding flights in the dark. Minka's mother was standing in the lighted doorway of her room. I could see now that she was very small indeed, but in a pleasing way. She was like a model of a dainty little lady carved out of china.

'Goot evening,' she smiled, and her eyes were twinkling slits. 'Come in, pleece.'

I shambled in with an air of unwillingness.

'Oh!' There was an exclamation of glad surprise from somewhere in the corner. Minka was sitting up in bed with a flushed face. 'I thought it was one of the girls,' she cried.

'It was one of the girls who told me.'

'How awful for you! Never mind. It's a schoolgirl habit to imagine a romance every time a boy and girl have two words together.'

'We had more than two.'

'*You* didn't.' She laughed mischievously. 'But if you're having a dig at me, it's true. I do talk, I must say.' She waved aside my protests. 'Sit.' She offered a chair by the bedside.

I sat down on it as if it was hot metal. Her mother had returned to her own chair at the window, through which she was making a show of looking. You felt her ears were pricked up for each word.

'Our home,' smiled Minka as she caught my roving glance round.

I smiled back in what was meant to be a reassuring way. The room was as poor inside as you would have imagined it to be from outside. It was obviously their one and only. You could have walked about five paces across its width and down its length. The ceiling was rather high, and made the place look roomier. A couch at one wall gave the finishing touch to its bed-sitting-room aspect.

'How are you?' I said, deliberately focusing my attention on her.

'I'm fine,' she laughed, and started coughing. 'It's nothing,' she said when it was over — and started coughing again. She had a paroxysm of it.

Her mother turned. 'You mustn't talk, Minka,' she said. 'I keep telling you —— '

'Be quiet, Mother. What do you think he's come here for — to look at my face?' She grinned at me:

'Mother's always at it. She means well, really.'

'Your mother only thinks of your good,' Mrs. Salomen tinkled across.

'P'raps I'd better go,' I murmured.

'No! There, Mother, see what you've done?' She got furiously flushed.

'There's always to-morrow,' ventured Mrs. Salomen.

'Maybe I'll be dead to-morrow!'

'Don't, Minka.' Mrs. Salomen was very moved. I could see there had been scenes of this sort before. I began uncomfortably to rise.

'Sit down!' ordered Minka. In a controlled voice she said: 'Mother, go to your window and keep quiet there.'

'You see?' Mrs. Salomen appealed to me timidly. 'That's

what I have to put up with. I'm only trying to save the girl going the same way as her father —— ' She broke off in alarm as Minka put one foot out of the bed. 'Please, my child, I won't say another word — go back. There, I'm at the window again, see? I won't look round once. Not once! See, I'm staying here. . . . You mustn't take notice of me' was her last appeal to us.

I got used to interludes of this sort on my subsequent visits. Minka was not in bed the next time I came, but her mother's fussiness was no less in evidence. Outside the question of Minka's health their relationship was very amicable. They were solicitous for each other in most matters. I felt I had brought an extra conflict into their lives; it was obvious that though Mrs. Salomen regarded — and welcomed — me as a potential suitor to Minka she was also jealous of the time Minka gave to me, She would sit by the window with half an eye cocked on us. She was ready to pounce into the conversation at the first opportunity, even though she had only the haziest idea of what we were talking about across the room. She would snatch on a word: 'A *pleeceman*, did you say? You would like to be a pleeceman? Yes, that's a good profession, all right, if you can only get into it.'

'Oh, Mother!'

'I only said something about a pleeceman,' said Mrs. Salomen hastily. 'Nothing more. I'm really looking out of the window.'

'Well, do so — and don't drive my guests away.'

'That's not fair,' Mrs. Salomen mildly protested. She appealed to me: 'Do I drive you away?'

'No.'

'There you are!'

'Mother, Mother,' sighed Minka. 'Do you expect him to say yes? Do go to your window, please!'

'Don't worry, I'm going.' She gave me a sly, mischievous

grin, as if we shared a common triumph over Minka.

The curious thing was that if Mrs. Salomen turned her head to interrupt — not with ordinary conversation — but with news about the doings of neighbours she had spied through the window, her reception by Minka was cordial. Minka was ready to permit her to break into the middle of anything provided it was with gossip. You could see this was an understood thing between them, for Mrs. Salomen lost her timidity when she had scandal to communicate and broke in boldly, knowing her words would be welcomed. They could both carry on for quite a time with one item:

'Sophie's with child again, I see, Minka.'

'Bit quick after the last one.'

'Exactly nine months.'

Minka grinned. 'Some people like to get things over in a hurry so that they can settle down to a peaceful life!'

'You'll make *him* shy with that talk,' her mother grinned across at me.

'He's got to learn things one day!'

They were completely in league against me in those moments. I could only grin sheepishly and say nothing.

I was now dropping in twice a week or so. I usually came after supper. I hadn't yet got to the stage of waiting for Minka at the girls' club and escorting her home. Once I did that I would be her betrothed in their eyes, no matter how platonic our friendship. As things were, anyway, I sometimes found a club girl or two in the house when I arrived and I didn't let my mind dwell on the kind of tale they would carry back.

Sometimes there was a neighbour present. She would cast curious glances at me from the window where she was sitting with Mrs. Salomen and I would catch a loud aside in Yiddish: 'Is it serious between them?'

Mrs. Salomen had obviously received her instructions.

'Just friends in the way young people are, you know,'

she would say with an attempt at airiness, but there was almost pain on her face at the self-imposed restraint.

The neighbour would nod understandingly but a trifle gravely. She had obviously not experienced such goings-on in her own youth. A male would have had to be a very slippery customer indeed to get away with 'being friends' after having shown his face in the home.

I hated it most when Minka's 'special' friend was there. I had known her by sight before. She was a girl who made up for her restrictions inside the club by overstepping all limits outside. Her voice was loud, her clothes gaudy and the make-up on her face seemed to have been splashed on from a bucket. I could never quite understand the basis of the relationship. I knew that Dora admired Minka for 'her brains'; but I never succeeded in finding Minka's reason for liking Dora.

She would come all over 'tactful' when I arrived.

'Well, I'll be leaving you two to it,' she would gush and then giggle as if at some very private joke.

'Don't be silly,' Minka would say. 'What for?'

'Well, you know the old saying — two's company, three's a crowd!' That was the kind of wit she had.

In the end she would be with us for practically the whole evening, carrying out the act of 'putting on her coat'. The 'tactful' ones often finish up that way.

The weather was getting warm about then and at Minka's suggestion we leaned up against the ground-floor shutters in the late evening. There was nowhere else to go. The squares were closed at night — presumably to keep the sexes pure. What it did was to drive them into dark corners for their love-making. England is the country of 'dark corner' love-making.

Minka and I were too young for that. There was also her mother to keep an eye on us. I discovered later that she had a relative or two that she visited only on the evenings I was absent. When I was there she would never leave us out of her sight for long. Even when we stood at the window outside she was down ten minutes after us, taking up her stand on the doorstep a yard away. She showed the same keen interest in the doings of pedestrians there as at her window. Every now and then she passed on a worthwhile comment or two to us.

I was never too comfortable there, what with Mrs. Salomen's curious little sidelong glances and my nervousness at the proximity of the youths at the corner. They disconcerted me much more than she. I caught bits of their talk sometimes that I tried to pretend to myself were quite different to what they had seemed to my ears. On one occasion there was a minor sort of scene when the cinema attendant came out chasing some urchins who had tried to get in by the back-door.

'Next time I ketch yer at these larks,' he shouted after them, 'I'll stick knives up yer . . . !'

Minka grinned at me. Mrs. Salomen called over, 'What does he say, Minka?'

I looked at Minka imploringly. She translated, still grinning, to her mother: 'He says he'll let them in for nothing next time they come.'

I couldn't help laughing — partly with relief, I suppose. Mrs. Salomen also laughed.

'I can just imagine,' she said.

Minka made a pretence of indignation. 'Then why ask? You're a nasty old woman.'

Mrs. Salomen giggled unrestrainedly. 'And you?'

They seemed to have a pretty low opinion of each other, I thought. They didn't mind it themselves. They were almost doubled up with laughter, the tears streaming from their eyes. I had to join them in spite of myself.

At about a quarter to ten Mrs. Salomen would call over: 'Come on, Minka — time for bed.'

'All right, Mother. I'll follow you.'

Mrs. Salomen hesitated for a moment or two. You could see her mentally weighing up the risks involved in our being alone for a quarter of an hour in the passage. But she had to make this one concession. Even in the most despotic homes it was the acknowledged right of a young couple to take their parting in privacy.

We rarely had peace for long. Mrs. Salomen would creep down the stairs and whisper startlingly in our ears: 'Hurry! *She's* got her friends here again.' 'She' was Mrs. Donaldson, the widow who lived on the second floor with her two children. When 'she' had 'her friends here' it meant that drink was the high-spot in the evening's proceedings and that there was all the danger of a violent termination to the party. It was customary for Mrs. Salomen and Minka to lock themselves in. Past experience had taught them that drink for some indefinable reason invariably revived Mrs. Donaldson's complexes about the Crucifixion. The flame of Christianity burned bright in her. More than once she had lumbered into the passage and loudly abused 'the Jew woman' upstairs. Mrs. Salomen had to admit that her apologies when she gained her sobriety next morning were no less vociferous. These were usually augmented with a peace offering in the shape of 'pie' or some other unkosher-like delicacy that offended Mrs. Salomen's food ethics. Mrs. Salomen inevitably had to accept. She could do what she liked with it afterwards, but to Mrs. Donaldson's face there was no accepting her sentiments without her food.

I became unemployed again. I was ashamed to mention it to Minka, but when I realised she would probably guess when I couldn't buy her some 'chips' on a walk or bring her a few chocolates on a visit, I thought it best to get in first with the news. I pretended to make light of it. She tactfully did so too. She even suggested I wait for her at the club's play-centre at five o'clock, where she looked after some children for an hour after school twice a week.

A Youthful Idyll

I had only intended seeing her home, but at her door her mother suddenly appeared and Minka said: 'Come in for tea. She's seen you, anyway.' She had instinctively understood my dread of meeting her mother that time of day. I had not exaggerated my fears: as I followed them in Mrs. Salomen said, 'Aren't you working, my boy?'

I groaned inwardly. Minka broke in sarcastically before I could say anything: 'Of course, Mother. He's just taken a half-hour off. Now, hurry with some tea and don't ask so many questions.' In spite of my extreme discomfort I was rather more grateful to her than otherwise. I tried to smile reassuringly in response to her mother's suspicious glances.

We sat round the grate after tea. I was moody and Minka sang to me most of the time. After an interminable period I suddenly looked at the clock in alarm. 'You'll stay to supper, of course,' said Minka quickly.

I looked confused and undecided and she gave orders to her mother without consulting me further. I put up no more resistance. Going home for a meal was never a pleasant prospect when I was unemployed.

As we munched our bread-and-cheese and pickles at the grate later there was a knock at the door and Dora came bursting in. It was never her custom to wait for a 'Come in'; she thought knocking first was as much as any one could reasonably expect from her.

I hadn't seen her for nearly two months. I noticed she had her hair coiled at the back in a grown-up way and she made irrelevant gestures with her hand to show off a ring on her finger.

'Ah!' Mrs. Salomen's welcome was the most effusive. A visit of Dora's always meant a bit of tittle-tattle from outside and she was allowed to join in as one of the company. She drew up her chair to the grate to complete the half-circle with Dora.

'Well?' Mrs. Salomen folded her arms in anticipation of

an exhaustive exchange of 'news'. Her little dark eyes twinkled happily.

'How's the dressmaking business, Dora? And everything else? They say you've left the club now that you've got a boy. Is that his ring? My, he must be fond of you!'

'Yes, I'm engaged. The ring cost fifty pounds!' A proud flush broke through her thickly-powdered cheeks.

'*Mazeltov!*' Mrs. Salomen's eyes twinkled without end. 'There's luck for you.'

Minka smiled her congratulations also. I tried it, but my intended smile somehow worked itself out as a grimace.

'Fifty pounds!' Mrs. Salomen was shaking her head from side to side in wonder. 'What's his trade, Dora?'

'He's a furrier in a small way.' She fondly patted the coil on the nape of her neck. 'Of course, my sister's ring was a dearer one than mine. But you know what times are now? Well, anyway, I wouldn't go lower than fifty. The men have got to pay if they want me!'

Mrs. Salomen joined in the joke with her and winked at me, as if it was something that ought specially to appeal to my sense of fun.

Dora cut in again with a trailing laugh: 'Sid and I haven't missed a Saturday out together for weeks. It's usually two-and-four seats at the pictures and a five-bob supper afterwards. There was only standing-room last week and he paid five shillings apiece for seats. He's a lovely boy!'

'I should think so,' sighed Mrs. Salomen. 'You're a lucky girl to get one so quickly. I'll be satisfied with my Minka to get engaged when she's eighteen or nineteen. A ten-pound ring'll do me —— '

'Mother!'

'What's the matter, you silly girl?' Mrs. Salomen grinned at me: 'You don't mind, do you? After all, you're fond of the girl —— '

'Mother!'

'All right, all right,' Mrs. Salomen said hastily. 'I'm not

saying any more. The subject is finished.' She grinned round triumphantly at each of us in turn. Only Dora responded.

I hated Saturday when it came. I had originally meant to ask Minka to the pictures, as in recent weeks. I knew she wouldn't go without me. I felt more wretched on her behalf than on my own. It was the only treat in the week for her. She and her mother were very poor. There was only a little pension in lieu of their dead breadwinner, augmented by a tiny grant Minka got out of her scholarship.

'I wish there'd been a social on to-morrow at the club,' I had said when we parted on the Friday. The season for them was over.

'Never mind. We'll have a nice time by ourselves. Mother goes off to Cousin Bayla on Saturdays.'

It sounded a little more promising than usual meetings of ours in the house and I turned up after supper in order to give Mrs. Salomen a chance of clearing out before me. She was still there when I arrived. She was washing up plates — dozens of them, it seemed — at the dresser near the window. Minka caught my curious glance and called out: 'Is this a sudden spring-cleaning, Mother?'

Mrs. Salomen's grin was more sheepish than mischievous this time. 'It passes the time,' she said.

'Aren't you going to Cousin Bayla's to-night?'

'Well — I — you're both staying in?'

'Yes.'

'I don't think I'll go,' said Mrs. Salomen with sudden resolve. 'It's really a long walk.'

'You've never mentioned it before.'

'Look at her,' Mrs. Salomen grinned slyly, 'trying to catch me out. Must I speak every thought?'

'Anyway,' she added, thinking of what she considered a really first-class reason for remaining at home, 'I must be here to see you have your throat-mixture and do your inhaling before going to bed.'

'I'm not a baby, Mother!' Minka's temper was slowly rising.

'Of course you are. Every child is its mother's baby till it gets married.' She grinned conspiratorially at me.

'Oh, you!'

'My poor child,' said Mrs. Salomen blandly, 'don't get upset with me. I know how it is for you. When there's no work, there's no money and one has to sit at home on Saturday in a bad temper ——'

'One more word from you, Mother . . . !'

'Shush,' said Mrs. Salomen hastily, 'I won't talk any more. Honestly. You two take no notice of me and enjoy yourselves.' She turned to the dresser again and left us to our misery.

I was only able to see Minka twice during the following week and on both occasions had to leave early on account of a mild renewal of her 'attacks'. She was spending days away from school and feared it would seriously handicap her in her career even if it saved her health. I felt sorry for myself. We had been getting used to seeing each other a lot. When I left her at night the pubs were still open and the ground-floor children were playing on the door-step of their house and waiting for the return of their parents. I wished Minka didn't live there. Poverty in the Jewish quarter was at least less spectacular. You didn't fear sudden outbreaks of violence from your neighbour.

I would lean up against a post across the road and wait for the ground-floor couple to return. They did so in the company of similar couples. I could hear them when they were merely moving shadows in the distance. They were bawling their lungs out; from past experience I knew it was supposed to pass for singing. Then I saw them in the light of the cinema. They were like strangers from a dark, stunted world. The men wore cloth caps well pulled over their faces and the women were beshawled, like mill-hands. They shuffled along with the gait of people whose journeys never take them beyond narrow streets.

They parted from each other with loud, hilarious cries, and laughter of the kind that usually accompanies smutty jests. The ground-floor couple remained alone. Their aspect changed. They hustled in the children impatiently and I could hear cries and wailings from behind their shutters long after the door had closed.

The light in Minka's window went out late. I could guess there had been trouble there, by the frequent hoarse coughing that reached me. I had learned from past vigils of this sort that Minka had a curious knack of controlling her worst outbursts until I left.

I listened a long time in the darkness. I had never felt so hopeless, helpless and utterly useless.

When we met on the Friday we arranged to make another attempt to have the place to ourselves the next day. We were more hopeful because Mrs. Salomen had now not seen her relative for nearly three weeks. When on Saturday, however, we saw her beginning to dust some furniture industriously at about eight o'clock, we knew the worst and by previous agreement between ourselves Minka suggested to her mother a combined visit to the relative by the three of us. It would be a change anyway and at least prevent the evening ending in a quarrel between Minka and her mother.

Mrs. Salomen tried to respond casually to the suggestion, but her pleasure was obvious in the rosy flush that came to her face.

'As you like,' she said, and added hastily, 'we'd better start moving if we want to catch her in.'

We went off. Mrs. Salomen ambled along about fifteen paces in front of us all through the journey. She probably thought herself the soul of discretion. We stared mournfully at her little back.

Cousin Bayla lived just beyond the district, in one of the few clean-swept streets that had gates to the houses. They were referred to as 'residences' on the landlord's hoardings. Hers was combined with a bakehouse in the basement where the family business was carried on.

We were opened the door by a woman below middle age who was dressed in an untidy dark pinafore and slippers. I thought she was the maid. When she kissed Mrs. Salomen and Minka on the cheek I knew that she wasn't. She was thin, with watery eyes and a nose that looked very cold — or perhaps it was inflamed. She inspected me critically. She was one of the first people ever to make me aware of my clothes.

She took no further notice of me. We were led into a well-lit room that was a kind of annexe to the kitchen and here after telling Minka to get herself and 'the young man' some tea she and Mrs. Salomen seated themselves at the other end of the table and began a conversation that had all the earmarks of one postponed from a previous visit.

I was relieved at her disregard of us and helped Minka prepare the table. I didn't mind being there provided the relative kept herself occupied elsewhere the whole of the time. It was a better room than most I had known. The walls were distempered in cream and the oilcloth glossy. Apart from these 'comforts', however, it was in as bad taste as any room in a poor home. The relative seemed to have tried to get all her belongings into it. The mantelpiece was crowded with knick-knacks, odd sorts of jars with names like *Westcliff-on-Sea* or *Clacton* on them stood around the dresser and sideboard and several faded photographs adorned the walls. The relative was obviously bent on exhibiting her history to every chance stranger.

Most of the pictures, I gradually discovered, were of the relative in different periods of her life. She seemed to keep a kind of check-up on herself. The largest was the one she obviously considered the high peak of the chart. It showed her in front of a photographer's landscape at the side of a bulky man with flaccid features and side-whiskers. I guessed he was her husband. Both of them were clasping the deck-rail of a non-existent ship. This was probably the nearest they had ever got to Foreign Travel.

Competing with the picture for prominence was an enlarged reproduction of an insurance society certificate in a beaded frame. The lower half was filled with a list of names; while the top half had a coloured drawing of an old bearded man ambling along with the aid of a staff into a golden haze of clouds. Two winged cherubs hovered about his head, leading the way. I gathered it was Moses off on the long trail to Heaven.

I stared at these things over and over again during tea. It was a curious miscellany to adorn a wall. When the relative moved her head I discovered a new addition to the collection. It was above the mantelpiece: a framed receipt for 'Fifteen Pounds, presented by our kind Benefactress, Mrs. Bayla Kleinberg, to the Breckley Road Synagogue'. The relative, it seemed, had her finger in many pies.

When there was nothing more to look at I gradually became aware of the relative's querulous tones. She was telling Mrs. Salomen of a sister of hers who was in the preliminary stages of arranging a marriage with a young man whose father kept a fried-fish shop. Mrs. Salomen was very sympathetic to the idea. 'Fish always does well,' she said.

There were some minor complications, according to Mrs. Kleinberg. The young man wasn't as 'normal' in mind as might be hoped for. 'Not violent, mind you,' hastened Mrs. Kleinberg in order to correct any wrong impression. His abnormality merely expressed itself in a few habits of a foul and nasty kind and inconvenient moments of half-wittedness. But — a 'loyal wife' could 'outlive' these.

'He's got a good heart,' said Mrs. Kleinberg vaguely. In

the absence of detailed evidence to support this theory I could only imagine it meant that he hadn't yet murdered anybody.

'Anyway, a fish-shop's a fish-shop,' said Mrs. Kleinberg, really getting down to brass tacks.

'There's worse things,' declared Mrs. Salomen.

Mrs. Kleinberg nodded forbiddingly and suddenly caught my eye. 'And what do you do for a living, sonny?' she asked with an icy cheerfulness. Her air was distinctly unhopeful. I could see she feared the worst.

I told her in a mumbling voice and when she nodded and slightly compressed her lips I felt I had been disposed of.

'You're always thinking of marriage, Cousin Bayla,' smiled Minka, trying to cover up my embarrassment.

'Naturally. And where would we be without it?'

'Well, where?'

'She's a child, Bayla,' Mrs. Salomen broke in hastily. 'Take no notice of her.'

'She won't *always* be a child,' said Mrs. Kleinberg, trying to look as if she was hinting at something very profound.

Mrs. Salomen shrugged. 'She's got time for a man yet.'

'*Sooner* done than later, believe me!'

'You needn't be so outspoken, Bayla,' Mrs. Salomen said coyly. 'After all —— ' She hesitated and looked in my direction.

'Well, a man's got to face the question sooner or later too,' said Mrs. Kleinberg, She imagined she was speaking in riddles.

'Let it be *later* if you don't mind, Cousin Bayla,' said Minka briefly. 'I think we'll go for a walk,' she added in a brighter tone of voice. 'The weather's nice out. We'll be back for you soon, Mother.'

I had never been so pleased at the sight of the street before.

It was no longer a problem where to spend our evening when I next went to see Minka. She was down in bed again and when her mother said mildly, 'You won't talk to her much, will you?' Minka didn't protest, but just smiled at me through her flushes. Her mother turned to the window again. I had the impression she had really left us to ourselves this time. As silent company we didn't interest her.

Minka and I just looked at each other. Her hand was on the coverlet. I took it and she changed the grip and drew my hand round her shoulder. I resisted in a mild way with a glance in her mother's direction. She shook her head slowly and placed my hand more firmly there. I had a vague impression of a death-bed scene. Tears sprang to my eyes.

We sat and looked at each other without stirring. She was staring at me as if tears were a curiosity she had not seen much of before. Just as I felt her becoming a blur before me she raised her hand and I felt a handkerchief dabbing at my eyes.

I felt a bit better afterwards. I wanted to speak very much, although I hadn't the faintest idea of what I wanted to say. She saw my eagerness. She shifted her head over to me. I bent down and whispered, 'You'll be all right soon.' She looked at me, smiled and nodded her head. She whispered, 'I'm going away again.'

I tried to look glad. I remembered she had been away twice to a home, but that the attacks had returned each time with a greater potency.

There was nothing more I could say. Her mother soon turned from the window and said, 'I think she must sleep now.'

Minka had already closed her eyes, but opened them again to look at me. I looked back and it was as though we exchanged a warm silent embrace. Mrs. Salomen stood by curiously. When she opened me the door it was in an almost awed voice that she said good night.

She was up from bed again within a week, but there was not the usual return to an appearance of health. I had to cut short my visits at about nine o'clock and each time there was a violent quarrel between her and her mother concerning Minka's right to take a parting from me downstairs. Minka inevitably got her way, but was loaded with scarves and pullovers for the journey, as if embarking on a polar expedition.

I noticed she never coughed when she was in the passage with me, although upstairs her cough had now a hacking sound and a handkerchief had always to be ready for her to spit into. She must have been a long sufferer to be able to exercise these restraints.

We didn't know what to say to each other. We just kept close and avoided talking in a too definite way about the future. I knew that she was going to leave me for a very long time now. I suspected it would be for ever. I was afraid to talk about it.

We would forget the time there, although Minka had promised her mother to return within two minutes. Mrs. Salomen had to come down to the foot of the stairs two or three times to call before we finally parted. She didn't creep right upon us unawares as in the past. Perhaps she had worked it out that we couldn't get up to much harm in the short time left.

I got the news of Minka's impending departure to the Home very suddenly and by post. I don't know whether she had deliberately saved it so as to avoid last scenes. The matter had been arranged and she was to leave in three days. l was to come along on the second day when she would be doing her packing.

I hurried round on the day I got the letter. I don't know whether eventually I should have found the courage to visit her against her wishes in this way, but I was saved the trouble of a decision. The window was dark. They were probably out taking leave of their few acquaintances and relatives.

I came along a little later than usual next day. She hadn't

wanted me to arrive in the middle of packing. I looked at the street with a kind of morbid curiosity. I wondered when I would see it again.

In the dim passage I almost collided with Ethel, the fifteen-year-old daughter of Mrs. Donaldson on the second floor. I had seen her around once or twice before. 'Oh!' she said, but didn't wait and ran past me sobbing: 'Ma's gone drunk again down at the pub, they say. Oh, what shall I do? What shall I do?' I stared after her disappearing figure, dazed.

They were still in the midst of packing, upstairs. Odds and ends of clothes were littered about the bed and couch and Mrs. Salomen and Minka were regulating the contents of a large open trunk. Minka was very flushed. 'The good-byes took longer than I'd expected,' she remarked. 'You find you've got a lot of friends once you're going to leave them.'

She kept up a kind of highly-strung personal chatter while I stood by:

'I'll take the playing-cards with me, I think. There's bound to be somebody who wants to play rummy.'

'These slippers will need mending in a few weeks' time, but I dare say I'll manage to find some kind of makeshift if I'm allowed to walk about. . . .'

Mrs. Salomen joined in the fussing also, as if the whole thing was the preparation for a holiday trip.

After it was over there seemed nothing definite for us to do. I followed Minka to a seat at the grate. Mrs. Salomen's eyes twinkled furtively at us as she fumbled about the room, straightening things up. Then she sat down at the table by the window, and said: 'It wouldn't have been a bad idea for a walk to-day, you know, if it wasn't your last evening.'

'I'm not stopping you,' said Minka shortly.

'Perhaps we'll all go?' said Mrs. Salomen with sudden brightness. 'Just a stroll near the door.'

'Go if you wish to, Mother, but please don't bother *us*.'

'I was only thinking of you,' Mrs. Salomen protested

mildly. 'You mustn't look so unhappy on your last evening at home.'

'Mother!'

'It's all right, really it is. I won't say another word if you don't want me to. I was only thinking of you —— '

Minka rose abruptly from her chair.

'Mother! Don't interfere, I said!'

Mrs. Salomen clasped her hands nervously. 'What's come over you, my child?' She appealed to me: 'Can't you be a better friend to her and stop her doing these things?'

'Mother. . . !' The word was a long scream from Minka's throat. I half-rose from my chair, but it seemed a ridiculously ineffectual action. Mrs Salomen was clasping her hands and moaning: 'Aren't you ill enough without standing there and straining your lungs! God, my only dear child to turn out a curse for me instead of a blessing. . . .'

'Shut up!' Minka's tones rose to a high shriek, which suddenly broke and released a fit of very violent coughing. I jumped up and put an arm round her shoulders as she spluttered into a handkerchief. Mrs. Salomen was still swaying her head from side to side at the table: 'My child, what have you done to your life and mine —— ' but she broke off sharply as the walls of the room trembled suddenly. There were loud voices from below and sounds of a body dragging itself up the stairs. Mrs. Salomen put a frightened hand to her cheek. There was a sudden barrage of thumping on the door. 'Hoi, you there, inside!' a shrill voice kept repeating in between the thumps.

'It's that mad *Goy* again,' whispered Mrs. Salomen. She seemed to shrink into her chair. Minka stepped over to the door with a handkerchief still held to her mouth and turned the key in the lock. The voice outside grew shriller with fury. 'Too prahd to speak to an old (*hiccup*) woman, eh?' It sank to a low sob for a moment. 'You wouldn't insult me if my Jim was aloive. Jim was a darlin', 'e wouldn't stand for me bein' insulted, no 'e wouldn't. . . .'

Minka called out in a hoarse, cracked voice: 'What do you want, Mrs. Donaldson?'

The thumping began again with a revived fury.

'Open the bleedin' door, will yer! It's yer Ma I want. 'Idin' from me, she is. I don't wan' *you* — yer bleedin' consumptive. . . !'

The thumping suddenly ceased a moment after. Minka got between me and the door as I tried to open it. Her face was white and dazed, like somebody hearing bad news. I felt very cold in my limbs. I heard Mrs. Donaldson shambling down the stairs, like a murderer stealing away from a crime. At the back of me came Mrs. Salomen's incessant moaning from behind cupped hands.

I led Minka back to her chair at the grate. I stood behind watching. Neither of them took any notice of me at all. After an interminable time Minka said, 'Please go home.' She didn't turn her head. I began to say something, but she cut in as if she had been expecting it. 'Please go,' she said. She sounded as if she was on the verge of screaming the place down.

I left quietly. It was my last sight of her.

I walked round the streets a long time. I didn't look at the people who passed me. Once I kicked against something and when it squealed I said, 'Sorry.' Then I saw it was only a dog. I wanted to pat its head to show my concern but it evaded me in fear.

I wasn't taking note of my direction, but every while I found myself back at the window. The light burned steadily all the time. When I returned for about the fifth time the window was dark; I felt it was like putting out the light of all life. I walked down the street in a blind fit of weeping.

PART THREE

CHAPTER 19

A Proper Shylock?

In my seventeenth year my mother began to hint more and more frequently at a certain unpleasant parallel between my father's life and mine. We were both indifferent to work; we shared a tendency to get discouraged easily. All too true. Personally, however, I was convinced that the resemblance was superficial. I like to believe that my own indifference at the time was conditioned by aimlessness. Whereas he wallowed in a fundamental inertia.

My mother made no allowances for these subtle distinctions in temperament. She was a bold, resolute woman herself. From her I must have inherited whatever sparks of ambition and determination animate me at times. From my father I have only inherited a desire to sleep at inconvenient moments and a tendency to think of suicide when trouble comes. I always think of the conflict inside me between the active and submissive as my inheritance from the one between my mother and father.

My father had every Jewish trait except the one the Gentile world has made into a legend: acquisitiveness. He didn't have even the acquisitiveness of the ordinary bread-winner. Only in my very early childhood did his 'business' enjoy a shortlived period of affluence — which as quickly expired with the progress of the War. The family like to believe it was his easy nature brought him down. It is true he didn't hoard and scrape: he spent the money while he had it and trusted to God to continue the munificence. He didn't know that men who trust to God outside the synagogue are doomed.

The blow had no worldly morals for him. To this day he goes round giving bits of his wages to beggars. He has an inconvenient disposition to see the other man's view-point. In a dispute over the rent his heart bleeds for the landlord's difficulties. Other people's troubles are the only things that move him to loquaciousness. It is an admirable ethical trait, but has always been unpleasant for his children. If people repaid the debts they owe him the family's problems would be unrecognisably minimised. He is convinced that his debtors suffer from a lapse of memory rather than one of conscience. He has an incurable and exasperating faith in human nature.

Privately, he must know as well as we that these debts are now 'bad.' We can tell that by the reluctance with which he goes to collect them. A 'bad' debt, by his queer standards, is one a month overdue. He begins to be embarrassed about mentioning it after then: it is vaguely bad manners, like reviving an old dispute. This has made him very popular with his customers. People like to buy from him. But the bigger his clientele grows the more his income shrinks.

I began to take a really critical attitude towards him only on leaving school; perhaps on account of being blamed for not making up for his failings. I was irritated at the casual way he let people treat him. He was 'Good old Benjamin' to every one — but it was rather a contemptuous tolerance on their part than a respectful liking. Even the local dogs sensed his inferiority. Whenever he came up the street they barked at him as at a stranger. He would pause and try to pat the head of the nearest dog. 'What's up, Jack?' he would murmur in the thin, querulous voice that came so oddly from his bulky figure. Dogs were the only objects he condescended to speak English to.

It didn't help at all. They cared nothing for his favours.

They would snarl and slip out of his reach in that special dog behaviour that is equivalent to the human 'Gurr, don't you touch me, you contemptible creature, you!' There was a look of pained puzzlement on his face. He couldn't understand dogs disliking him when men didn't. But to my eyes, as I watched such a scene, it seemed to explain everything: 'Even the dogs,' I thought bitterly. I cursed him for the heritage I imagined he had handed on to me.

Our growing poverty perturbed him less than any one in the family. He had never been self-indulgent, even in his 'prosperous' days. His apparel in all weathers was a waistcoat and trousers. He only wore a tie at weddings. The youngest working member of the family had to knot it for him: the task was beyond his own comprehension; he thought it needed an 'education'. I myself served him from the age of fourteen to seventeen. I don't know what he did before my elder brother was born. Perhaps he didn't go to weddings. Or perhaps it was fashionable to attend them without neckwear. I am not well up in the changing customs of weddings.

I have a memory of regular quarrels taking place over his clothes. He couldn't be persuaded to vary them even when funds permitted. He had known nothing but ragged pantaloons in his childhood, and since coming to England couldn't get over the wonder of a pair of trousers. These and caps were the sole articles of dress you could get him to replenish. He only wore a shirt and waistcoat as a gesture to society.

Until a fairly late age I was accustomed to thinking of him as a jolly figure of fun. I was proud in knowing that his bulky person in its cap, waistcoat and trousers was a familiar sight in the neighbourhood. In period dress he might have been something out of Dickens. It was only that he didn't talk much — and Dickens' characters are very verbose. When he returned from work we used to jump on his lap. We liked sitting there, it was very ample like an arm-chair and could hold three or four of us at a time. We would sit playing with his face. It fascinated us, there was such a lot of it. He let us do what we liked. He only minded when you poked a finger in his eye.

At the time I was only vaguely aware of the family's declining fortunes. I knew there was something in the wind by the quarrels that began to occur regularly between him and my mother. I noticed he went to bed immediately after. He went to bed more and more as I grew older and by the time I was an adolescent life for him was a perennial bed-time.

I didn't attach much attention to it in the early days, because he was engaged in various ventures. These I thought to be the many pies in which he had a finger. In reality they were the last few dice he threw.

One I clearly remember was his horse and cart. It was the most opulent of possessions then. I used to wait for him to return from his deliveries, so as to get a ride to the stable afterwards. I was popular amongst the local children. 'Gi' us a lift on yer dad's cart,' they begged me. I dispensed free rides like a producer presenting complimentary tickets for a circus. Every evening they waited round the door for my father to drive up. Then the clamour started. My mother would come rushing up the stairs to chase them away — unless by then my father had allowed the lot of them to clamber on to the van. He often did this when he had no other load. It would go careering down the street, with its cargo of children yelling and singing like a charabanc outing.

The horse-and-cart business only lasted a year — and my popularity vanished with it. In that time my father had had four different horses. Each was stolen in turn. I dare say it was partly due to his carelessness. He hadn't even changed the stable after the first theft. He didn't want to hurt the owner's feelings. He just went out and bought another horse. He did this four times. He named each horse except the last 'Dick'; the last one he called 'Tom'; he hoped there would be a change of luck with the name. But 'Tom' fared no better than the rest.

After the last theft there was no more money for horses — or perhaps there were no more horses left. He had to 'open up' again in the local market. Here he sold at different periods hardware, fruit, and fish. His 'business' was a cross between a shop and a stall. Architecturally, it was a square hole bored in the wall and fitted with a counter. Behind this he served his customers. The counter was very important. Without it he would have had the status of a pedlar. As it was the property could legitimately be called a 'business'.

I used to come out and watch him for a few minutes on my way home from school. He seemed a tremendously important person to me behind that counter. I wished he would keep it long enough for me to join him there when I left school. I asked nothing more from life.

When he wasn't too busy I would go over and he would let me duck under and stand beside him while he served. I was very proud to be there. I had a lofty contempt for the people on the other side.

He was making less and less during that time. The quarrels between him and my mother were increasing. When he brought home his earnings to her on Friday I would listen from the grate, where I was playing. Neither of them minded me. They had a queer notion that anything outside the school curriculum was gibberish to a child.

'How do you expect to live — giving credit all over the place!' she would exclaim.

'You can't let people starve,' he would murmur in his high-pitched, apologetic voice and shrug his shoulders.

'Starve? Your customers' children will have more to eat than yours — you can be sure!'

'Nonsense,' he would say, but you could sense the discomfiture and half-guilt in his voice. Perhaps it wasn't so much that he believed in the decency of people, as that he *wanted* to believe in it. The truth might have been unpleasant. He didn't like unpleasantness.

'What can you do with the man?' It was her last desperate appeal, made to the four walls of the room as well as to him. Neither they nor he responded.

'What can you do with the man?' became from then on her eternal cry — directly transferred to me in my adolescence, in the hope, perhaps that it might bring more tangible results than in the habit-hardened case of my father.

It was the beginning of a real landslide into poverty. We got poorer and poorer over a period of a dozen years. The War had been our peak. We were then considered to be doing 'not so badly'. It is true that a younger brother of mine contracted asthma through being taken out of his bed at night during an air-raid and still suffers from the complaint to-day at the age of twenty-five. For that matter we might all have contracted cancer. It wouldn't have lessened people's envy, provided we were doing 'not so badly' — that is, managing to eat and pay the rent. There is no other kind of 'success' in a slum neighbourhood.

The War had been well over before I began to hear rumours of the now-familiar legend of my father's folly. I felt a secret pity for him during the better part of my schooldays. It was when I attended a Central School at the age of twelve that I became critical of his appearance. I was wearing my first soft collar. I gave up passing the market on my way home. The sight of him irritated me. His curious apparel was no longer a symbol of fun for me, but of barbarism.

For a little time he still had my sympathy when my mother picked on him. I was also amused at the way he ended a quarrel by going to bed.

I was no longer so after leaving school. Particularly in the slack seasons. I knew that my mother's incompleted rage would exhaust itself on me. I gradually assumed the role of his scapegoat. I was expected to make a success of all the things he had failed at. His name was mentioned among us only rarely, like a near relative gone to the bad. Sometimes he got an inkling of things and would complain that 'nobody told him anything'. We had a radio remaining to us from better days and he began to take a sudden interest in it, although he couldn't understand half that came from it. He liked listening to the news bulletin. I used to watch him through the scullery window, sitting alone with the head-phones pressed to his ears. The words meant nothing to him, but he liked the deferential tone of the announcer. He regard-ed the news as a personal message. It was as if the announcer said: 'Listen, Benjamin, this is for you. There's a deep depression over Iceland. Pretty bad, eh?' He thought the announcer was the only person who treated him decently. He was quietly pleased after a news bulletin, as if coming away from a heart-to-heart chat with a friend.

At seventeen I was duplicating his quarrels with my mother. Like him I was continually being reminded of people who had 'made good'. The neighbours would assemble in the house and talk about me as they had used to talk about him. Except that in my case they did it in my presence. When they didn't talk about me they talked about people who were 'doing better' than me. They specially liked to bring instances of somebody who had had 'a stroke of luck'. This embraced anything from winning a sweep-stake to 'being left something' by an uncle who had died of cancer.

I heard a lot of this kind of talk during my third slack season. There was one lengthy period in which gossip history was unwittingly made by a youth across the way who had had a windfall of '£200 damages' for a finger lost at work. 'Wouldn't mind losing a *hand* at that price,' said a very fat woman at least once a day in my presence.

I suffered a genuine guilt at the time in knowing that I was sound in limb while cripples were making the money.

CHAPTER 20

Class against Class

O UR street, like the larger world, was a 'divided' community. The divisions were merely not so fundamental:
which means, in plainer words, that somebody as respectably
well placed as a bank-clerk would have turned up his nose
at us all. In their innocence, however, this didn't prevent
various inhabitants turning up their noses at each other.
Class identity is something people only recognise when it
is forced on them by a class catastrophe. Ordinarily each
man likes to think there is some one on a lower step in the
social ladder he can look down upon.

Welk Street was no exception. It flourished on its multi-
tude of 'differences'. The people on our side tended to be
more neighbourly with each other than with the people
across the way — and distance was not the reason. The fact
is our homes were more substantial. We had a basement as
well as the two floors above; they only had the two floors
and no basement. To clinch it, there were more children
on our side — the extra space no doubt encouraged this
extravagance.

Trades mattered a great deal. We were a miscellany with
a dominant flavour of tailoring. Only a couple of people
stood out supreme; one was Joe, the confectioner. His
house was actually pokier than most, but the front parlour
was a 'shop' and that made all the difference. He was the
street capitalist. People envied him everything but his wife:
she was the snag — Joe had had to accept her along with
the 'business', and there were some who thought her parents
had got the best of the deal. She was most unwholesome. In

her first week in Welk Street they had labelled her 'Dirty Kate'. She had a large, amorphous figure and streaky yellow hair that for ever strayed about her face ('to hide it', as people said). She walked with a shuffle that put your teeth on edge. Around her she kept a coterie of large and aged yellow cats that were apparently there to fit in with her personal colour scheme. You might easily have taken them for her offspring. She had no children; it was rumoured that Joe 'wouldn't risk it'. That didn't make him less enviable. A business is a business. An ugly wife? — after all, it's only the nights that you have to get through.

The tailoring workers were a class on their own. They even looked alike. The majority were small, round-shouldered men with an eternally weary air, who appeared from their houses startlingly spruce and clean-shaven every Saturday afternoon. By Monday they would be their old selves again. They were week-end Cinderellas.

Their habits were identical too. They smoked a lot and sat outside their doors in summer. They were the most solid, dependable strata in the rock of our street society. Most evenings would find them with the family. Even a call on a relative was a rare adventure. Apart from the seasonal vagaries of their trade they were regarded as model husbands by the women.

Among the remaining assortment of cap-makers, cabinet-makers and the like my father was the one market worker. Market workers are not judged by their work, but what they make out of it. Consequently my father was respected up to the end of the War and increasingly despised after it. The ostensible reason was his physical coarseness. It hadn't attracted any notice in his prosperous days: his coarseness was presumably then a charming eccentricity, like that of an aristocrat who belches at table. People only began to mark his coarseness when it was accompanied by poverty. Everything was then laid at its door. What after all but failure could be expected of a man who never wore a tie, and shaved only on festivals? Then there was his choice of clothes. Full of significance. He wore a cap, for instance. You never see elderly Jewish men in this undignified apparel. The trilby is mostly favoured. My father had probably picked up the habit from the fish-porters at Billingsgate. It is rather strange that he never picked up any English from them; their mutual business had to be conducted in a kind of pidgin Yiddish. A great many of the Gentiles who did business with our people were compelled to adopt this form of speech. Washerwomen, in particular, had to use it a lot. One who came in to work regularly for my mother was quite fluent. She eventually gave up English altogether, or perhaps she forgot it. I used to listen to her chasing away the cats in the back-yard in a most admirable Oriental invective.

My father was really not very differently placed from the ordinary sweat-shop worker: it is a commonplace that the market and sweat-shop worker mutually envy each other largely through ignorance of each other's trades. My father was always harping on the stability of people with a 'real trade in their hands' — irrespective of the fact that at the time there were close on two million of these people with 'a real trade in their hands' signing on at the Exchange. The sweat-shop worker talked perpetually of 'the adventure of trading'. Yet before him too was the spectacle of 'adventurers' who hadn't moved an inch in a dozen years from their pitch in the gutter.

There was a stigma attached to the poorly flourishing market worker that the equally poor sweat-shop worker somehow escaped. It can only be explained by the brutishness of the market worker's job: the kind of habits he indulged in followed as a consequence. He was irreligious and undomesticated. His own family bored him. He preferred the rough talk and manners of his friends in the Yiddish restaurants. These places took up the market worker's leisure; and because of the irregularity of their hours and work market workers had quite a lot of leisure. My father was rarely with us of an evening. He was in bed if it was to be an early market next day, or at the restaurant if not. The restaurant gradually became associated in our minds with his failure. During the War we were prepared to believe he was there discussing 'business'; but in the absence of any real business since, we could only regard it as blatant loafing.

Most of these places were shunned by respectable Jews. They were open all hours and usually invaded by the billiard hall 'boys' on their way home at dawn. This was largely because of an exclusively Jewish menu. As 'exiles', these were the only places where the 'boys' could get Jewish food. It helped them not to miss their homes.

Their mass patronage consequently put a mark on the Yiddish restaurant and gave rise to certain suspicions about my father. His business had only to slump at the end of the War for people to 'put two and two together'. They probably thought he had gambled it away. It was much more convenient to accept this as a reason than to delve into the complications of economics.

His persistence in the habits that were associated with his 'downfall' was sufficient to push him down to a near ground-level rung on our social ladder.

We had no master-tailors to give our street distinction. But we had the nearest thing to it and as he also possessed a passable wife his standing eclipsed even that of Joe the confectioner. Mr. Svetchkin exhaled an almost frightening respectability. He spent his day 'supervising' the back-parlour that he and his wife had turned into a millinery workroom. Here sat four busy 'hands' and Mrs. Svetchkin. Mr. Svetchkin had once been a trousers machiner but had nobly sacrificed his own ambitions for 'the business'. The business was a notoriously 'good thing': not only had it released Mr. Svetchkin from a tiresome sort of labour, but it also enabled him to send his son Saul to college. This last was Mr. Svetchkin's real glory. In my own embittered view Saul seemed the dumbest thing I had met with in years. The more I saw of him the more I became convinced that Mr. Svetchkin was defying nature by keeping him at school. He ought obviously to have been doing a healthy eight-hour day digging up some road. This he would no doubt have had to do and still be doing had his mother not opened a 'work-room'.

He was an only child and modelled both mentally and physically in the spit image of his father. This presumably was what specially endeared him to Mr. Svetchkin. At sixteen he had the same rotund, barrel-shaped figure and the same pompous air. He was slightly the more objectionable of the two: his father's pomposity was cultivated and consequently a never too certain quality; whereas with Saul it was a heritage. At sixteen he had already bought himself a walking-stick to augment his confidence. This walking-stick accompanied him everywhere except to bed.

Saul was the Great Example for the street's mothers. He enjoyed a vague and undefined reputation for 'cleverness'. There was no particular evidence to support this theory except that Saul had college fees paid for him while the rest of us worked for a living. At the elementary school he hadn't even had the superficial intelligence to reach top class. If it had not been for that work-room he might have remained an unimportant blot on the landscape to Welk Street mothers. The work-room made all the difference to his standing: he was that interesting and unusual thing, a 'College' boy. His 'college' consisted of short-hand classes. Nobody had heard of any other kind of education. Cambridge and Oxford were popularly thought to be rowing teams, in the same way that the Arsenal is a football eleven.

Saul was one of the bugbears of our adolescent lives. It came to be common amongst mothers who wanted to reprove their children to say: 'Saul Svetchkin wouldn't do such a thing'; or, 'Saul Svetchkin — there's a parents' blessing!'

He and I attended the same club for a year, during which time he got himself to be the most detested person there. His very life was threatened. Once he nearly got himself lynched by referring in the hearing of a number of us to a club boy who was educating himself by evening classes as 'only a workshop fellow'. People who gained by striving what he had gained by privilege were the special target of his hate. He enjoyed a certain immunity from assault due to 'a weak heart' — a myth of his own invention that nobody thought of testing by asking him to show a doctor's certificate. Eventually some one tried the experiment of beating him up and when he didn't die immunity was withdrawn from him and he had to behave himself like anybody else.

His father played the pest with rather more success. He had been one of the people you had to keep your eyes open for when as children we kicked a ball about on the Sabbath. Any forbidden act he caught you at would be sure to reach home before you did. He had an observant eye for all the wrong sort of things. He gossiped enough for ten people and represented his busy wife in housewifely circles; it wasn't easy to pick him out in one. His voice was high-pitched and his figure, clad in the appropriate clothes, might well have belonged to the feminine bearer of a couple of offspring and another 'on the way'. He was the street Oracle. 'Mr. Svetchkin says . . .' was the local Ten Commandments.

Of all people he had to choose my mother for his audience. I frequently returned home to find him laying down the Law of Life. He treated children as if they were deaf-mutes: he never addressed them. He only talked about them. He would occupy the best chair at the table, one short leg crossed over the other, his waistcoat open to the third button up to 'give him room', and his large trilby set tentatively on his head as if placed there a moment before by the shopman. He would wag a gentle forefinger all the time he talked. He scarcely smiled and you had the feeling that an actual laugh would wreak irreparable damage to his face. Perhaps he felt this too, for he never took the risk. He had dull, heavy-lidded eyes that looked as though they were perpetually encountering unpleasant sights. Other people's children were obviously one of them. 'Tut, tut,' he would say painfully if he was present when I walked in after my usual bed-time. My mother needed no more encouragement: she would start upbraiding me and finish up with the inevitable reference to Saul. She and Mr. Svetchkin had a special sort of dialogue for these occasions. It went on such identical lines each time that you might have thought they had rehearsed it, like a cross-talk turn:

'A nice time to come home — ask Mr. Svetchkin if Saul comes home at such times!'

Needless to say I didn't ask; but that didn't prevent Mr. Svetchkin from answering me:

'Well, what do *you* think?' And he gave a deprecatory shrug.

'I should say not!'

This conversation was very puzzling, since they were obviously both in agreement from the beginning. But they seemed to want to make sure.

'You see, Mr. Svetchkin, that's what you have to put up with from children.'

'Well, I don't know.' He would nod his head, metronomically: 'Some children are like this, some are like that.' He thought he was being tactful.

My mother sighed. 'You're lucky with your Saul, Mr. Svetchkin.'

'I'm not grumbling,' Mr. Svetchkin said modestly.

The Svetchkins' house was the end one on the pavement. It was the quietest too. The door wasn't perpetually open for children to run in and out of. It remained that way even when Saul was a child. He had his definite hours of play, like a house-dog. On the stroke of seven he disappeared inside its portals and Mr. Svetchkin came out to put up the shutters. He performed this job very meticulously. You had the impression that it was important that no air should get through the cracks. When he had finished he glanced round the street, as if taking a last look at the world before hibernating for the winter.

Sunday was the one day in the week that he kept the door open, but he effectively discounted this by blocking up the passage with his person. It was observation day for him. He stood watching child-like activities through his disapproving eyes, mentally collecting material for the coming week's tale-bearing. The rare Sundays that he was taken abed with a cold were followed by a comparatively quiet week for us at home.

Mr. Svetchkin was a law to mothers. He was supposed to know everything. They referred to him as a 'well-read' man. This meant that he bought the Yiddish newspaper regularly, instead of casually like the others. He would 'explain' the political situation to people: he had a first-class memory for the leading articles. His verbosity was very impressive. 'He *can* talk', people would say, and they thought they were paying him a compliment.

He played a significant part in undermining my father's position at home. He had his own methods. One was to time his visits to coincide with my father's absences. The contrast between his fireside domesticity and my father's loafing in some strange restaurant pointed its own moral. It was a puzzle how he succeeded in avoiding my father if you ruled out spying. He never failed, however, to comment on his absence. 'Where's the old man?' he would ask in pretended surprise and my mother's replies used to be an evasive, 'Oh, out somewhere'. But Mr. Svetchkin's repeatedly sympathetic 'tut, tut's' gave her more confidence. Her evasions gradually changed to a self-pitying: 'Well, where do you think?' There would be 'tut, tut's' of a rather bolder kind and an exchange of glances very much in the style of close friends mutually commiserating over a particularly unpleasant 'skeleton in the cupboard'.

When I grew older and began to resent Mr. Svetchkin's familiarities my mother would retaliate: 'If your father was a man like him *you* would have turned out different!'

The more I saw of Saul the more glad I was that my father wasn't a man like Mr. Svetchkin. But he wasn't very satisfactory like himself, either. The knowledge was a source of bitterness.

CHAPTER 21

There's a Good Time Coming

THE same year witnessed the 1929 slump. For the younger people it was the climax of a fruitless era: many streamed out of the ladies' trade and into the market as pedlars; others forsook the market for the menial and under-paid jobs in the ladies' trade. The victim of the frying-pan invariably thinks the fire a cooler place.

The influx to the ranks of the unemployed outnumbered both sections. The Exchange was no longer a place you sidled into with a furtive glance up and down the street. It was continuously besieged. You met all sorts down there both in the way of clothes and of accents. The democratic spirit communicated itself even to the desk-clerks, taking the edge off their brusqueness.

Making a claim now involved a lengthy vigil. Even when you got to the counter you often had to await the convenience of a scribbling clerk. Embittered wits had a habit of indenting their epitaphs on the desk with a penknife: 'Died While Waiting' faced my eyes morning after morning. It was not encouraging.

Having to wait there so long got people into the habit of treating the place as a club. They did everything there except gamble. Talk buzzed incessantly. Predominant among the subjects of conversation seemed to be the bad state of trade, the failure of the existing government, the prospects of horses, dogs and football teams — variated by stories of human interest, such as, 'what happened to a bloke over in Poplar who tried workin' and drawin' the dole'.

It was a very unpretentious basement. Its single purpose

was blatantly clear. The walls were dark, bare and cold. A notice-board provided the only bit of colour: it was spattered with 'warnings' — conspicuous among them one giving the name of a man convicted for making a false claim. The only other poster was a recruiting one. It showed a happy group of soldiers holding their haversacks ready for departure abroad. It made me want to travel too — but not with the Army.

The older youths would make for the Tower of London afterwards. The air was fresh and you could sit on a bench facing the river. On a fine day the birds twittered in the trees and it was the nearest thing to the country. The tourists bustled around all the time. When they came across a 'sight' you could hear the snick of their cameras and their rapturous comments. Most of us merely guffawed. We had no eye for the architectural wonders of our country. Its poverty had blinded us to all else.

When it was too cold to sit for a long spell we wandered through the grounds. Sometimes we paused to watch the soldiers drilling or playing football in the spacious Moat. They were there on most days, presumably with the object of showing the public how grand Army life was.

At twelve o'clock we went to view the speakers on the Hill. This was the once-famous gallows. In these enlightened days it served as a kind of open-air club for the unemployed.

It was also a bit of a market. Every day a man walked up with a large case, set it down, and began booming: 'Friends! I have with me here the finest remedy for disease of the scalp. Tried and proved perfect by Royalty,'— and a few bald-headed men would assemble round hopefully.

A considerable amount of heckling went on at other platforms. Notably the religious ones; there was usually a policeman or two around these. The most uneventful were those addressed by the quacks. Day after day a thin under-sized man offered to turn every one of his audience into a modern Hercules for the 'price of a bottle of beer'. He might have had more luck actually selling beer instead of 'body-building mixtures'.

At dinner-time we would drift homewards. On the way back alongside the railings that skirted the Tower number-less beggars stood in the gutter. Officially they were pedlars. Each one had something to sell — in compliance with the law. It varied from matches to picture-postcards. Vendors of the latter kept up an untiring serenade:

'Nice view of the Tower, sir. Only sixpence, sir. View of the back-ground half-price, sir. The most beautiful building in the world. . . .'

Even in the short winter season rush that came to the workshops a little later there was no forgetting the slump. The beggar became a familiar caller, like the coal-merchant or char. The slump had turned him into an established institution. Beggar didn't mean 'vagrant' any more, but 'unfortunate'. Occasionally it would turn out to be an aged tailoring worker reduced to begging through incapacitation. Some of the men would maybe recognise him as a colleague from former days and there would be a shaking of heads and a dipping into pockets and when he left the vast shadow of an impending doom would hang over us all.

Itinerants of a new kind greeted you on the way home to dinner: genuine musicians made redundant by the talkies. They were travelling orchestras — but with an audience now of household drudges instead of pleasure-goers.

The Gentiles deteriorated perhaps the most alarmingly. Many in our street had made ends meet with 'hopping'; supply exceeded demand there too. Jews who had previously taken in a Gentile for the washing applied their own hands to the tub. They also saved a penny by getting their own children to light fires on the Sabbath, hoping God would understand.

The new scourge spared nobody but the pawnbroker.

CHAPTER 22

Art for Art's Sake

EIGHTEEN can be the most tragic age in a working youth's life. What is he to do when a 'street corner' life loses its charm — leaving him with nothing fittingly adult with which to replace it? Every working youth has the problem to a more or less conscious degree. In the vast majority of cases there is a realistic submission to fate and the mind coils up inwards, like the spring in a clock. All growth stops. The pursuits of eighteen remain the life-long pursuits of manhood.

A small minority are constitutionally incapable of compromising. They turn what is called 'queer'. They undergo long intervals of unsociability — or what are known as 'moods' among the poor and 'temperament' among the rich. They behave unconventionally. They may read books surreptitiously, or adopt some other 'intellectual' pursuit. They may do neither of these and merely keep their hair long or wear a bright-green jacket for work.

I did some of these kinds of things myself, but in a mild and rather sporadic way. I never kept to one of them for long; poses can also become a tedious routine. There is nothing intrinsically dynamic in them to keep them interesting.

'Eccentrics' are not uncommon in the East End. Sometimes they are thwarted artists; sometimes social misfits with a stunted capacity for living. To the population in common they are an unvarying collection — with the label *queer*. They are local characters. People point them out in the street: 'See that long-haired fellow?' (A significant finger is applied to the forehead.) 'Some say he's supposed to be clever.' This last is added from a sense of fairness rather than conviction.

The 'queer' are also the lonely. Often if you get to know them well enough you find them charming. They are merely not good mixers — or perhaps despise ordinary company. I think I was free from the more extreme of these manifestations. I had had too long an experience of club and street life not to be a good mixer when I wanted to. The trouble is that I wanted to less and less. Complete lack of a private life was producing an anti-crowd complex in me.

It was during this psychological crisis of sorts that I met Ephraim Wise for the second time. The first occasion was at the club I belonged to at the age of sixteen. We had never had much to do with each other there. Like most people I had vaguely thought him a half-wit. He had all the appurtenances. His movements were clumsy, his speech halting and in his eyes a kind of 'grin' for ever lurked, as if he enjoyed some private chuckle incomprehensible to the rest of mankind. When you caught his eye you thought he was laughing at you. But the feeling was dispelled after one word with him. He was obviously ill at ease in human company; you were left to conclude he was slightly crazy.

I hadn't given him much thought at the club. I was too active during my attendances to have any time for 'drifters'. Wise, as I recall, was very much of a 'drifter'. I don't know why he joined. He took no part in any of the activities, but flitted through the premises like some pale, restless ghost; he had a perpetually vague air of searching for something. His appearance was very crude. He was below middle height with the frame of a labourer. He looked the sort of person who continually stumbles into people. His face too was strongly moulded. Only his expression sometimes gave him away — it was a boy's expression, uncertain, irresolute. He might have been thirty, or he might have been sixteen. I only knew he was sixteen because of his membership of the club. His physical make-up was as contradictory as I later on found his mind to be. His jaw was large and aggressive; but above it his eyes were a gentle blue and his forehead high. You couldn't make up your mind whether he was a sheep in wolf's clothing or vice versa. This was probably why he never suffered the usual persecution of a 'misfit' in the club. Nobody cared to risk the bashing he looked at least fifty per cent capable of giving.

At a close scrutiny his skin was very elastic. His face looked as though it could be as mobile as a clown's; but it was always impassive, largely I think because of his tiredness. He gave the impression of a dynamic force being relentlessly worn down. Navvies sometimes look like that after a day's work. Wherever you came upon Wise he had an air of having just arrived from walking the streets. Even in crossing a room he did so with the weary mechanical shuffle of the tramp.

I gathered he had joined the club for 'company'. He didn't make much use of it — or perhaps he wasn't given the chance to. He remained only a short time. He drifted out as he had drifted in: anonymously. Had I given a thought to him I would probably have imagined him flitting through similar places, unnoticed and unwanted, a wanderer in the eternal search for human kindliness.

Our recognition two years later was mutual.

'Hallo,' I said. At that moment he wasn't an 'outcast', but a friendly face, for he was obviously unemployed too. I wondered that we hadn't run across each other before. You meet everybody in the slack season.

'Hallo,' he murmured and I wondered what he was so amused about; till I remembered that the 'grin' in his eye was a permanent affair.

'No job?' I said, trying to work up some cordiality.

He shook his head. The 'grin' was disconcerting me in spite of myself. It was as though he saw through my attempts at making conversation and was determined not to help me out. But he showed no signs of wanting to pass on.

'Well,' I said. 'Going this way?'

He nodded rapidly a number of times as though I had made a most provident suggestion and fell into step beside me. A silence grew between us. I found a sudden interest in the sights around and thought he was pretending the same — until I snatched a glance at him from the corner of my eye. His gaze was fixed in front. It was hard to persuade yourself that he wasn't enjoying a private joke of his own.

I thought I would try him.

'What's funny?' I said conversationally.

He looked at me in surprise, but the 'grin' was still in his eye.

'I thought you were laughing?' I said.

He burst into a boisterous laugh. You would never have thought anything so considerable could come from him.

'Don't you ever laugh?' I said.

This time his laughter was very prolonged. It was spontaneous and infectious laughter. It was difficult to believe such a pathetic-looking object could enjoy anything so whole-heartedly. I felt immediately at home with him.

'You walk like a tramp,' I remarked.

He agreed with alacrity: 'That's what they call me at home. Fat Rachel invented it.'

'Who's Fat Rachel?'

He regarded me for a moment, as if surprised that I didn't know her.

'She's my sister.'

'I've got a sister Rachel,' I said inconsequently. 'She's not very fat, though.'

'She's not like mine,' he said with a kind of dark knowledge.

'Don't you like her?'

'She amuses me.'

'You must enjoy home life,' I said a trifle enviously. I was beginning to find my own rather harassing about then and had vague plans of leaving.

'I don't live there,' he said, and at my look of surprise gave his loud, joyous whoop again.

Doubts about his sanity returned to me.

'Out of home, eh?' I said. He wasn't exactly an encouragement for me to go and do likewise.

He nodded rapidly several times. He was obviously very pleased about it all. We had just reached the top of the turning I had to take for home and he came to a halt with me. He stood there like a friendly dog that hopes it won't be dismissed.

'Having any dinner?' I said. I hadn't the faintest idea what I would say if he answered no. An invitation was impossible; I was getting my own food only grudgingly.

'I'll eat later.' He grinned reassuringly at me. 'I'm staying with somebody.'

'Good!'

We looked at each other. 'Signing on to-morrow?' he said, fidgeting a little. I had already discovered that his difficulties in speech manifested themselves mostly when he had to take the initiative.

I nodded, but was silent.

'I'll hang around for you.'

'All right,' I said doubtfully. He raised an awkward hand in greeting and I watched him shamble off like a big tired dog going nowhere in particular.

We met a couple of times more during the week. I discovered that he wasn't signing on at the Exchange, but was merely there trying to establish a claim to money that he considered was owing to him from past stamp contributions. I didn't learn any more. I myself hated discussing the workshop outside it and he presumably was not favourable to discussion of any sort. There was mostly a silence between us, but not an uncomfortable one. I liked having him by my side: though he didn't talk much himself he was very responsive to remarks addressed to him. I discovered that his laugh was the big human thing about him. He hadn't the sardonic quirk or the rest of the stock-in-trade of the worldly. He either enjoyed a thing or he didn't. When he didn't he was as impassive as a statue; but when he did his laughter was a joy to hear. The tears streamed copiously down his face. You simply had to laugh with him. That laugh, as I found later, was the essential child in him that all the world's blows could not destroy. It was his secret genius and because genius can only be crushed by death it had to die with him.

I first knew he was an artist when we sat on a bench in the Tower. I didn't pay much attention when he began sketching the people around. Many do that sort of thing to pass the time. When I glanced over his shoulder I saw that his sketches were different. They weren't the usual conventional profiles. They were people caught in characteristic attitudes. After that I stared all the time at his large clumsy hands that were so dexterous with the pencil.

'Good,' I said admiringly.

'It's nothing.' I sensed a bitterness rather than modesty in his tone.

'You can do better, I suppose?' I said.

'I've *done* better."

'Well, where's the work?'

'Under the bed at home,' he said, without taking his eyes or pencil from the pad. 'For Fat Rachel to use any time she wants to light a fire.'

'Gee!' I was really shocked.

He shrugged almost imperceptibly.

'Can't you sell 'em?' I said.

'Tried to. But I can't carry round that junk with me all the time. I'll do better pictures soon.'

'You will?'

'Sure. I'll get going again.'

'It's hard for artists.'

'D'ye think I left home and took all this trouble for nothing?' He turned a hard stare on me.

I said nothing. He returned to his sketching. I felt as though I had insulted him. I watched him in furtive bewilderment.

I saw it was best to accept him at his own valuation. He responded sympathetically then. I learned that many of my first impressions of him had been wrong. He wasn't a half-wit, for one thing. He might not have been quite 'normal'; but it was the abnormality of a thwarted artist he suffered from, not of a half-developed youth. He hadn't been entirely a 'drifter' in the old club days. He had been in the midst of pursuing an artistic career. It was his first period out of home. It explained his short stay at the club: he always returned 'Eastwards' when his luck gave out. He only expected to sit on benches with me until he 'got his strength up' again.

He had been staying all over the place in that time. Sometimes it was in lodging-houses, sometimes in an odd corner of an old acquaintance's room, sometimes even in the streets. Wherever he was he had always managed to tramp to his parents' house for a few meals during the week. He did this more for his mother's sake than his own. It was the one way he could assure her of his safety.

Gradually, as I learned to know the rest of his family by having them pointed out to me in the street, I began to understand a little more his uncompromising stand. There was his father and a brother besides Fat Rachel. All three were in some way the spit image of Wise. Yet different! You noticed it the longer you stared at them. It was the kind of difference that sometimes exists between an ape and an ugly man: the difference between the primeval and the civilised in the same species. That is the nearest I can get to it. They all had Wise's uncouthness and his slightly 'half-witted' expression ; but they left one with an impression of a hard, impregnable stupidity. They lacked that something that made you warm towards Wise, that something that came from his hidden genius and was his humanity as well. I think it was in their eyes. They were the eyes of people whose thoughts are for ever on the 'main chance'.

There was no denying that Wise had inherited much from them. He had also, however, inherited artistic genius from some mysterious other source. This was the conflict within him.

To his people he was a problem — but not a psychological one. He was merely the ordinary problem of the 'no-good'. That was their explanation of his artistic ambitions. He was 'too big for his boots'. They felt he had no right to be 'different'. People with warped lives will forgive you anything but being different from themselves. They will deny it as long as they can: label you 'no-good', 'snob', 'stuck-up', and all the rest of it — until you prove your difference. Then they will hate you with a mean, murderous hate. That is the greatest honour they can do you. It is the reward of the artist who rises from adversity. Death cheated Wise of this reward. He never got beyond the stage of contempt and sly sabotage.

That was later on. Meanwhile I could experience his unworldliness at first hand: he was the butt of all the miniature bullies and Napoleons of municipal life. He had only to walk into the reading-room of a library for the official's eyes to light up as he visualised a pleasant afternoon throwing him out. Bumptious little busybodies that he could have trod underfoot talked to him as they liked because of the authority that backed them. They were merely taking advantage. He didn't know how to talk to people. It is only fair to add that he didn't care to know. Occasionally in going to meet him at the library I would stumble into him half-way down the stairs. He would face me with a large sheepish grin. He knew I disapproved of his submissiveness.

'Well, what's up now?' I would say.

'Was just havin' a word with somebody —— '

'And so the librarian thought that a good reason for

throwing you out? You come up with me and we'll see what happens.' I knew he would be safe then. I wore better clothes and I had a businesslike air in the library. I usually wrote there. Like all snobs the librarian over-estimated people he couldn't quite place.

Even then it wasn't easy to get Wise to return. He preferred to avoid unpleasant people. He saw no satisfaction in standing up to them. His egotism was solely concerned in expressing itself artistically. He was indifferent to persons. Only pictures mattered.

I gradually pieced together his history since leaving school. The first two years had been spent in a workshop. He was put there on turning fourteen. There was no particular reason for this choice of trade except that his father was in it himself.

What Wise endured during that time can only be imagined. It was no wonder he preferred to it the life of a vagrant. His fingers, that could be so facile with a pencil, exhibited their inherited clumsiness with a needle and thimble. He was very backward in his work. Added to this his shyness and halting speech must have brought him endless chaff from his uninhibited Cockney workmates.

Some time after his father gave up the workshop for the adventure of going into business 'on his own'. This business of Mr. Wise's was rather difficult to define. He sold different commodities every day. The nature of these depended on what he 'picked up' nosing round the markets. He had a small shop-front in which herrings and cami-knickers lay side by side in apparent amity. Wise took me along for a look one day. As far as I could make out his father seemed bent on ruining Woolworth's.

Wise then put his proposition: he wanted six months' freedom to attend an art school. If, after that period, he failed to win a degree that would guarantee him a career he would return to the workshop without a murmur. This was an old bone of contention between him and the family. He was again refused outright.

What particularly annoyed Wise was that, parallel with this meanness, the old man was continually throwing money down the drain in purchases of a quite unremunerative kind. 'Bargains', he called them. One day he would arrive home with a sackful of buttons which there wasn't the remotest chance of selling, the next day with something equally worthless that had taken his fancy. He seemed to spend half his time in the markets buying up things that other people didn't want. These purchases rarely turned out to be 'bargains' — except to those who had succeeded in palming them off on him.

Wise had to take action on his own. He spent one more season in the workshop, saved some money by stinting himself of week-end pleasures, and joined the art school by paying down a sum on account.

During his attendance there he endured his share of humiliations, as he was destined to do in whatever sphere of life he entered. Most of the students were wealthy. When I had known him for some time he told me how on one occasion when an appeal was made in the classroom by the teacher for the loan of a car every hand went up but his own! He was continually coming into the limelight this way.

The persecution at home didn't at all let up during this period. They considered they were making 'sacrifices'. They let him know it, particularly at meal-times. It served them the purpose of both letting off steam and saving money on food — for they certainly ruined his appetite. There were rare times, however, when impressed in spite of themselves by his industry and dogged persistence they restrained themselves and let him eat a meal or so in peace, scenting the possibility of his future greatness and wishing to be 'in on things' should he emerge, after all, a 'successful'— i.e. well-paid — artist.

At the end of the first term Wise was short of three pounds for the second term's payment. An appeal to the family was received resentfully. What did he think they were — million-aires? Fiddling with paint brushes while they all slaved their guts out working for him!

They were hopeless. But perhaps what pained him more was the attitude of the school authorities who, while praising his work, refused to use their influence to get the small fee paid for him, or alternatively, to allow him free entrance to the school for the remaining term.

Before giving up he made a last desperate effort that was typical of him. I have hinted, I think, that while he was pliable and easy to handle in everyday matters, this was reversed in the sphere of his art. He seemed to know in-stinctively that society kept him where he was by an ad-ministrative violence and when he wanted anything he in turn made his assault on society by a reciprocal violence. He simply ignored his expulsion. . . .

The method of continuing to attend worked for a little while: it was like attacking an enemy with surprise tactics. But inevitably he was discovered there and repeated warnings given him to leave, all of which went unheeded — until he was thrown out bodily by the porter. Even after this he succeeded in getting in once or twice (in later years he developed this knack to an almost ghost-like perfection), but his appearance was conspicuous and the whole staff were instructed to keep a look-out for him. Under such surveillance even a genuine ghost would have found entering the school no small task.

The pressure had naturally increased at home. By now they were convinced he was a failure. They insisted on his return to the workshop. This was too much. He felt the new life within his grasp. He was determined to follow up his 'start'; but it was a programme clearly impossible to carry out at home; which was why he left. He intended to try wresting some sort of living by his drawing, with the object ultimately of getting back into the art school to complete his studies.

All this had taken place before I met him again. I gathered he was as far away as ever from his goal. It was true that he had 'contacts'; but he was continually losing touch with them owing to the expense of phoning and the great distances to their houses. This was one of those periods. He was doing what he called 'resting up', in preparation, presumably, for another series of long tramps to the West End.

I tried to persuade him to eat at home oftener now that it was so accessible. I was unsuccessful. It was too close a contact — as later even his daily meal became. He couldn't stand the nagging. His sister was chief offender. She was twenty-three, a large, clumsy, unattractive girl without friends and with diminishing prospects of a marriage that at the best of times had appeared only hazily on the horizon. Wise was an ideal target on which to vent her repressions and disappointments. If she was there when he came for a meal what he ate would be fairly certain to find its ultimate haven not in his stomach but down the drains on his way out of the house. He had to be extremely hard up to eat there even once daily. He could be seduced from the prospect by a 'treat' of anything from a cup of tea upwards.

Knowing it to have been his routine of living for so long I could now understand the impression I got of a corroded vitality. He must have been endowed with an extraordinary physical toughness. His 'toughness', in fact, became a legendary thing; it so disarmed both of us that when he collapsed in the end it was as much a shock and surprise as would have been the spectacle of the Houses of Parliament crumbling before one's eyes. I can never forgive myself for not foreseeing it. I took too much notice of his boisterous optimism — I believe I came to regard him as immortal. Yet signs of the approaching catastrophe were clear. Apart from his eternal air of physical weariness there was the pallor of his face, a pallor that verged on grey. His hair, too: it was thick and dark and combed back — but when you caught sight of him from behind you were shocked to discover a bald patch. Its area grew ever larger during the time I knew him.

He of all people was least concerned about his physical condition. If somebody had made him a present of a studio I feel sure he would have spent his life in unceasing work there, without even a thought of meals. He was unworldly to a degree that was nothing short of appalling. I have known him give his bed-money to a street musician standing in the gutter. Once I gave him an old suit of mine that I had discarded in quite good condition. After waiting three weeks for it to appear on him, being given vague pretexts during this time of 'some mending' he had to do on it, 'pressing', and other adjustments that I was quite certain the suit was in no need of — I finally dragged out of him the admission that he had given it away to a passing beggar he had taken pity on. I was dumbfounded. Then I grew angry, hurt, resentful. What did he think *he* was — a millionaire? I gave him a long lecture on the necessity of being 'practical' and he listened speechless and uncomfortable, shambling along shamefacedly beside me. I believed I had impressed him. It wasn't long before further criminal acts of generosity on his part convinced me that the 'shamefacedness' he exhibited on these occasions was not on account of his action, but merely embarrassment at being 'told off'. I realised that if I lectured him until Doomsday he would never comprehend the slightest reason why he should not make a gift of my clothes to passing beggars. He would have been a positive danger to himself with a fortune.

He was a very difficult person to help. His habits, like everything else, were contradictory. He rarely washed — but would not sleep in a fivepenny bed at the Salvation Army because he said it was 'lousy'. It had to be a Rowton House bed at a shilling, or the streets. You couldn't despise him for it. He was prepared to suffer for his principles. Once I took him to the barber's for a shave and he ran out of the place after the first 'once-down' of the razor on account of being unable to stand the barber's face peering into his own.

It was no better with food. He was a vegetarian. To this he attributed his beautiful white teeth on which he never used a toothbrush. Tactfully I refrained from asking why the diet hadn't worked similar wonders with his hair. But there it was: he was an undeviating vegetarian. People sometimes tend to be the products of their diet. Wise, if you covered up his eyes and hair, might easily have passed for a well-battered turnip.

It was difficult enough to help him without these stipulations. I was only a little more fortunate than he in that I was getting bed and board at home. I would run across him late at night and find he had nowhere to sleep, but was unable to do anything about it except give him a shilling if I had it, or run round to some one I knew to get it. Once or twice I sneaked him home with me for a place on the kitchen sofa — *sneaked* him home, because my people would have liked nothing better at the time than to pounce on me for any real or imaginary misdemeanour. 'Bringing my friends home to be kept by them' is how they would probably have described it.

One day he took me along to his lodgings. They were at the home of an old school friend in Stepney Green. He was allowed to sleep on a 'bed' that consisted of two wooden forms placed side to side and to use the room as a makeshift studio during the day. It was a bare place with only a mirror on the wall. It had once been handy as a box-room.

There he commenced a 'head' of me. It was in watercolours that he had been made a gift of. He painted me five times in what ultimately proved a futile attempt to capture a certain 'something' in my face on paper. The fifth was the best effort, although still unsatisfactory to both of us. To my inexpert eyes it looked like a grinning close-up of some deep-sea denizen.

It turned out to be a timely contribution to an exhibition.

Art for Art's Sake

We were both elated when a large and distinguished-looking invitation card arrived from an address near Cork Street. We set out to make a day of it at the gallery.

On approaching the place I lost my nerve a little. I anticipated quite a trying time persuading the attendant that Wise was no tramp but an actual exhibitor. Ultimately it was I who presented the card — implying that I was the artist and Wise a man hired by me to carry away any purchases I might make.

Inside we went through the conventional rigmarole of looking round. We pretended to forget our special purpose in coming. Perhaps we were trying to lengthen the delights of anticipation instead of losing them by making for our picture at once.

We grew a little restive after viewing two rooms without a sign of it. Pretence was discarded and we quite openly ransacked the building. We ultimately discovered the portrait in a box-room adjoining the exhibition rooms — together with bits of rope, stray chairs, and some of the guests' overcoats. . . .

'Well,' said Wise at length, 'it was *done* in a box-room, anyway.'

I was much more disturbed than he.

'It's an insult,' I kept repeating. 'They'd no right to take it if they were already full up with pictures. Fancy, a boxroom?'

'They might have put it in the w.c.,' said Wise.

I didn't know whether to deride or admire his optimism.

I now saw very little of him. He was off on his 'calls' once again, encouraged no doubt by his 'acceptance' at the exhibition. I usually met him after one of his rebuffs and got the story from him. He had now reached the stage of breaking into people's houses. Sometimes it worked; most times not. Bernard Shaw on such an occasion treated him with courtesy and gave him ten minutes for a drawing, but no 'commission' followed it. Another equally famous

writer, whom he confronted in his own hall under the eyes
of a mystified butler who had 'seen nothing' pass his way,
brusquely ordered him out with the information that he
only made appointments through his secretary.

Once he enjoyed a period of guerrilla warfare with the
editor of a well-known artists' journal. Getting past the
porter was nothing; it merely hadn't occurred to him that
during the long journey upstairs there was time for the
porter to warn the editor by phone. Which is what the man
did. However, the bolted editorial sanctum only put Wise
off for a matter of seconds. He prowled around until he
found a back entrance and surprised the prematurely
triumphant editor at his desk. . . .

These tactics, the tactics of desperation, didn't get him
any further than before, nor did they intimidate hard-
headed (and perhaps hard-hearted) editors. All that
happened was that these people had locks fixed all over
the place and tried to employ porters with eyes at the back
of their heads. For Wise their antics were a source of amuse-
ment as well as of aggravation. He couldn't get over the
idea of editors barricading their homes against him as
against a fierce and hungry wolf.

He left writers alone after a time and concentrated on
theatre people. His methods for making contact with them
were varied. Sometimes he waited for them at the stage
door, sometimes sent them a letter in this style:

Dear Madam,

I would gladly pay you £200 for the privilege of painting
your portrait. But as I haven't got 200 farthings at the
moment I would be very grateful if you would allow me to
do a portrait for nothing, which I shall be only too glad
to buy back from you for £200 when I am a successful
artist one day.

Yours hopefully,

EPHRAIM WISE.

Results, again, were mixed — with the balance not in his favour. There were firstly the people who were tickled at the idea of being 'portraited' by a slum artist — 'Wise of Whitechapel' they nicknamed him. He made a little money, but failed so often to follow up his contacts, for they were busy people and he couldn't afford the numerous telephone, correspondence and fare demands on his pocket that pursuing them involved. Nor did tramping down to places like Chelsea improve his hand with the brush when he arrived there at his sitter's house.

The overwhelming majority quite frankly disliked his face, his manners and his bluntness — particularly his bluntness. He had a habit of drawing people as *he* thought they looked and not as they liked to think they looked. One famous actress, whose perpetually flashing smile is no doubt calculated to pass her off as sweet-and-twenty, went into a terrible rage when revealed in her forty-odd years on Wise's canvas. And *that* commission was lost.

There was one notable exception in a retired Army man with whom Wise indulged, during the whole of the first sitting, in a mutual slanging match. The major had strong political views that were the very antithesis of Wise's own. Wise let him know this plainly. That started it off. They slandered each other's favourite 'parties', slandered each other, then went on to exchanging oaths of the juiciest kind, as if trying out a private language of their own on each other. Wise did his share without taking his pencil off the paper. The major must have led a very boring life, for he asked Wise to call again.

This was Wise's 'flush' period. He rented a room for himself in the East End for a few weeks and slept in a real bed. He also ate quite a number of meals. Previously he had had a theory about one meal a day being sufficient for a man, a theory that I had always suspected of originating in necessity rather than conviction. Now he proved me right. He walked into every restaurant he passed during the day

175

for something to eat; but his stomach had been brought up on routine of a different kind and couldn't adjust itself to the sudden change. He usually finished the evening by spewing the whole of the day's food down the drain and so ironically enough carried about with him a stomach as empty as it had been in the most acute days of his privation.

Perhaps this was the most eloquent sign of all that time had done to him, for his stomach — like his teeth — had been the pride of his physique. I realised that a once-robust youth of nineteen was rotting before my eyes. He seemed to get an inkling of it himself, for when it was followed by a turn of 'bad luck' once again he fell into what was for him a mood of pessimism and complained of his health. Even then he was not abnormally worried, but resentful and puzzled, rather like a man who experiences a headache for the first time in his life. He talked of getting 'better', so that he could pursue his contacts with the same fervour and energy as before.

It was mid-summer. He proposed attaining his 'convalescence' on the road. Once before he had done a similar tour in the winter and survived it, so that he calculated this one to be a relatively easy matter; he also intended earning himself something 'on the side' by sketching any motorist who gave him a lift. He saw himself returning both rejuvenated and remunerated from the journey.

CHAPTER 23

Art is Long, Life is Short

LIFE changed for me a good deal in his absence. It didn't change for the better; it merely changed. I had left home and though to get away from domestic crowding and squabbling was a relief, the lonely moments brought remorse. It was a new conflict of a kind. I wondered how I would stand up to it when the first delights of independence palled. The urge to do something with your life is much greater when you are alone. I had got as far as knowing that I wanted to write. Wise's presence would have been a great encouragement to me and not the deterring example that might be expected. He had a way of convincingly turning existing values upside down. I was beginning to believe him the sanest man alive: he was merely out of luck because he lived in a mad-house.

I eagerly awaited his return.

He wrote me frequently. His letters came from different places along the English coast and from their tone I could see that he was amusing not only himself but a large part of rural England. There were snapshots of him sitting half-clothed on the beach and consuming a litter of assorted vegetables, surrounded by a crowd of urchins and village ancients who watched him as warily as though he were a strange deep-sea monster washed up on their shores. There were descriptions of the furore his appearance had caused in remote little villages on the south coast. In one little hamlet in Devon the shocked inhabitants rushed for the village policeman, and Wise was hurriedly 'deported'. He seemed to derive immense fun in leaving excitement and turmoil behind him. He particularly chose remote little spots where he could shock the inhabitants with his appearance.

Then I didn't hear from him. I began to wonder whether, during his misadventures, he had suffered a more serious penalty than 'deporting'. . . . One night there was a knock on the window of my 'digs' and through the pane there stared at me Wise's huge grinning face, warm and grimy — but healthy and alive too. I had never seen him that way. When I opened the door he strode through the passage and into my room like an empire-builder glad to be home from Rhodesia. He was bronzed, tough and confident. He looked thirty years old, but the thirty of a man advancing to his prime — not to middle age.

I was terribly pleased about it. We divided up the bedclothes and a place was made for him in another part of the room and we thought it all very amusing. He chuckled all the time like a great, happy child — the more so when I took his sweltering shoes and stockings and placed them outside on the window-sill for the night. I don't know what the people opposite thought, but I preferred risking their contempt to death by asphyxiation during the night.

We awoke very late after talking most of the night.

'Well, what plans have you got?' was the first thing I said. He looked so fresh and energetic that one felt he must surely have plans, both ingenious and numerous.

'Nothing special,' he said cheerfully. 'I must start hunting up people.'

'You mean, go for long walks again?'

He laughed.

'You've had some good practice now, anyway,' I said.

'That's right!'

I pretended to share his optimism.

The most disappointing and heartrending but not so surprising thing to me in those first weeks was not the slow response of his 'contacts', but the alarming rate at which his new-found energy departed. A few journeys on foot to Chelsea and he was once again the tramp of previous days. It was really serious. Nothing showed so conclusively the toll his mode of living had taken from his health. One after-noon in the East End I tried to hint at this. He was very derisive.

'I'm only nineteen,' he said. 'I'll pick up like anything when my luck changes.'

I had learned enough not to question the inevitability of his 'luck'. I tried a new direction.

'By the time it comes', I suggested, 'you might be too worn out to do much with it.'

He shook his head. 'I'll never be too worn out to paint if I get the chance.'

'But it'll be a pity if in the middle of a promising career you die young because of early privations.'

'I'll still have got more into my short life than a lot of people get into a long one.'

There was an improvement in his hopes if not in his actual circumstances in the coming days. He was 'nursing' a contact in Hampstead. Because of this he foisted himself on an old acquaintance near Charlotte Street. He considered himself quite lucky, although his share of the 'lodgings' consisted of a blanket on the floor at night. There was now less walking to do for his calls. I was glad about this, but was anxious for the time when the little money he had made from his tour gave out and he would have to walk down to the East End for meals.

'There's no fear of that,' he said cheerfully. 'I'm going to pull off this commission all right.'

I had to admit he had more substantial grounds for thinking so than usual. He had made a very auspicious start with his client, being permitted to do a preliminary drawing that he would be paid two pounds for if it was approved of, with probably the commission of a real portrait to follow. He had obviously made an impression. He himself was amused rather than unnerved at the test he had had to undergo. His client had been sceptical and suspicious at their first meeting; he was a famous musician and hadn't taken very seriously a request for a sitting on the unusual terms of 'two pounds if you like it, nothing if you don't'. Wise, however, was no easy person to get rid of once he had gained access to a house and as the client had no ex-Guardsman in his employ to deal with this sort of intruder, he attempted to solve the problem his own way. This took the form of trying to discredit Wise's *bona fides*. He was taken for a viewing of the private gallery of Old Masters upstairs in the house in the hope that he would reveal his ignorance. The result was very disconcerting to the musician and landed him still further under Wise's obligation: Wise proved to be well-informed and critical.

Wise never forgave him these suspicions. The sitting that followed was not a very sociable affair. The musician's attitude was incurably patronising all the way through and Wise's response was a parody of it: in the field of his art he had an objectionable habit of treating people as his equals. When the musician asked him conversationally, 'What's your father?' Wise amiably told him and in return asked, 'What's yours?' This kind of exchange didn't improve their relations much.

Wise brought round the drawing for me to look at when it was completed. It had only taken two sittings. 'It's an easy two pounds earned,' he said.

'It's good,' I admitted. 'But it's not a very flattering picture, is it?'

'You mean the eyes?' He burst into a joyous chuckle. I began to laugh with him. I wondered how he'd had the nerve to reveal somebody's character in their eyes in front of their own faces, so to speak.

'What does your client think?' I asked.

'He didn't specifically mention the eyes. But he thinks I ought to touch it up a bit. . . .'

I could well understand his not wanting the picture as it stood. Those eyes! Sly and cunning, they were. The owner of them would, if he were invited to somebody's house, find on his arrival a sudden panicky rush on the part of his host to lock up the silver.

'What was the idea?' I said.

'He looked suspiciously at me all through the sitting — so I drew him as he looked. It'll teach him to trust people next time!'

'I hope you haven't done for yourself now.'

'Not if he's got a sense of humour.'

'People's humour doesn't usually extend to themselves, you know.'

'Well, it ought to.'

'That'll be no comfort to you if he doesn't commission the portrait.'

'He can't be so nasty.'

I shook my head at him. 'Wise, Wise,' I said. 'If only you lived up to your name.'

He was merely amused.

It will never be known, I suppose, whether he did actually destroy for himself the possibility of a commission; for the musician, it turned out, had quite legitimately been scheduled for a South African tour shortly. He could promise nothing until his return. Perhaps there is an indication of the way the land really lay by his refusal to pay for the picture. Yet perhaps it is merely an indication of his meanness and of nothing else! One feels that in conscience bound — as a 'sportsman', that is — he ought to have given Wise the two pounds for at least living up to his claims and proving his ability. However, he didn't do this; and Wise could certainly not ask for it in the terms of their arrangement.

The musician's departure was a real blow. Wise had banked on the two pounds as his minimum 'success'. Now he had nothing at all to see him through the coming winter, nor had he anywhere to stay, for the man whose floor he was occupying at night intended to go abroad.

My offer of hospitality was of no use to him. Not only did I now live in a district that was neither very accessible to the East End nor the West End, but I had only the dole and he definitely refused to share my food.

He returned to the East End one day, to that old box-room 'studio' in Stepney Green. It was always open to him if he cared to spend his nights on two wooden forms.

This period marks the 'old age' of his young life — the period in which man, as depicted in the 'Seven Stages', begins reversing in gear. Wise fell back into a kind of adolescence; an adolescence that was not a natural stage on the journey up the heights of human development, but a degenerating 'adolescence', a milestone down the slope to ultimate extinction. It was characterised not by unquench-able optimism and unfailing energy, but by a sense of impending defeat and a relapse into slothful living. Food he scarcely ate now. His mother's allowance was supervised, making it impossible for her to give him any meals but those the family approved of: this meant a few vegetables left over from *their* meals. He ate less and less at the home — I discovered later that he had sometimes been existing on an orange a day. He didn't grumble. I don't think he cared; he was probably in the first stages of his madness. I should have suspected it by some of the nonsense he had begun to gabble at our meetings, but it was difficult to be sure, for he wasn't a coherent talker at the best of times.

He didn't come to see me much. It seems he spent most of this period in loafing the streets with an acquaintance of his boyhood days. Perhaps that was the most tragic of all signs. Artists in humble circumstances frequently suffer from having to consort with people who, though their hearts might be in the right place, have no minds worth speaking of. Wise had such a 'friend', a dried-up, wispy young man who found books and art boring and who much preferred having 'a good time' — a term he used to describe his one weekly cinema jaunt for sixpence and stolen moments spent in a dark back-street with an atrociously scented female.

I found myself with a terrible conscience about Wise. Whether I liked it or not I was the only person in the world who realised his position. Other people merely found him a nuisance. Only I knew; and I was doing not an iota about it. I couldn't even take him along with me to look for work. Ironically enough, now that I had at last got him to the stage of admitting that he ought to pursue his art as opportunity offered and not as inclination demanded, his physical condition had degenerated to an extent that made him unfit for work of any kind. He obviously needed a year of good and effortless living.

Now late in the day he realised this himself. There was no more boasting of his fine teeth, his 'toughness' and superhuman endurance. We schemed how to achieve this necessary 'holiday' for him, but nothing came. I suggested he should try getting work with his father, who now had a second-hand clothes stall in the market. It would see him through for a while.

The terms offered when he eventually approached his father were merely board and lodging but no money. He refused. 'Living there is no gain to me,' he told me. 'It would only make me iller.' I didn't really feel justified in persuading him otherwise. The offer was quite obviously made to him not on the basis of his worth but on the basis of his starvation.

The main prosecutor of this cruel piece of blackmail was Wise's brother, a tall, gawky lout two years younger than Wise. The years Wise had spent in pursuing artistic ghosts had been used by this young man in strengthening his position in the family, making himself indispensable to his father and especially to the business, until now he virtually controlled it. He hated Wise more than any of them. Yet he betrayed his essential weakness in a most pathetic manner:

like the sister, he too was friendless, and when he wanted to go to the pictures on his weekly half-day he had to fall back on begging his brother's company. Had it not been for this regular 'treat' Wise would have seen few films in his life.

Outside this special occasion his brother only had hard words for him. More ruthlessly even than his sister and father he tried to break his spirit. Being harsh to his mother was one way. She was a weak, timid woman with no say in the house. He made her spend long winter days at the stall and then put on his brother the onus of this necessity. It was the thing most calculated to pain Wise — ill-treatment of his mother. She was really very fond of him. I was with him once when we passed her in the street on the way to the baths (accompanied by the younger brother, who always escorted her there to see she spent the threepence he had given her on its legitimate purpose). She was a small, stocky woman with hair turned white and the gentle, persecuted expression that I had always seen her with in Wise's drawings. He only stopped to speak to her for a moment. (His brother stood surlily aside.) You couldn't doubt the strong affection between them. They chuckled happily and touched each other's faces with fond fingers as they exchanged loving words: it is the only moment I have ever known Wise free and uninhibited. He pinched her cheeks softly and caressed her hair as you do a baby. You could see in that moment how directly his adolescent clumsiness and restraint came from starved affection. With love instead of hate around him his uncouthness would have fallen from him like a decayed cloak.

It was a puzzle to me how a fond mother could tolerate her son being treated the way he was being treated. It was only later I learned that Wise had concealed from her most of the stark realities of his condition. She knew vaguely that he 'went about' and knew 'lots of people' and it was easy to convince her that in this way he kept himself fairly well-nourished.

Art is Long, Life is Short

There was another three months for me on the dole and I decided that job-hunting would have to wait until Wise could be safely left to himself. I was very uneasy about him. He looked more weary than he had ever looked before. He was evasive to all questionings. I couldn't find out when he'd eaten, what he'd eaten, or even *if* he'd eaten.

But I was glad to be with him, also because of my writing. I would be able to show him my efforts. I soon saw I was to be disappointed. Instead of taking a lively interest in his surroundings or sketching while I wrote, he sat staring into space. I realised that to ask him to read anything in that condition would be unfair. I did my writing quietly. When I had finished the little I could manage for the day we would get up and go for a walk. It soon became a habit of ours to get up and go for a walk before we had intended to, for Wise would start a sudden and unexpected discussion of my work in the middle of the library and it was best to anticipate the attendant's order to leave than to wait for it. These outbreaks in the midst of a stony indifference puzzled me. I hadn't encouraged him at all. What complicated things more was that I could not understand a single point of his remarks. I didn't know whether to think he was 'above' me or quite definitely crazy.

His presence at the library began to harass me. When he started to talk I prayed he wouldn't do it for long, or talk of matters outside the sphere of literature. I even welcomed the intrusion of his 'friend' Sam to ensure this. When Sam came into the library I knew I would have a period of peace. You couldn't discuss literature with him around. You couldn't discuss anything at all much. He sat beside Wise, sharing his indifference and his stare into space. Once when we left the library together and Sam took his departure from us at the corner of the street I said to Wise curiously: 'Do you like his company?'

Wise shrugged. 'He's a good-natured fellow.'

'What do you talk about when you're both together?'

He looked at me slyly. 'Masturbation,' he said. 'It's Sam's hobby.' His delighted roar echoed along the pavement.

When there was no Sam present he was off again on his favourite tack.

'Look,' I said one day. 'I don't say I can write. But I hope I'm capable of seeing a point of view when it's put to me. The fact is, I can't make head or tail of a word you say!'

He was silent. 'Take no notice of me,' he said at length. 'I'm a bit wonky these days.'

'I'm sorry. But if you're *really* trying to put forward a point of view?' I added hopefully.

'Well,' he said, and he seemed to rally himself. What I'm saying is . . .' His humility had quickly been submerged by a revived belligerency. We had the whole thing over again.

The main plank around which the structure of his argument was built was the technique of the novel. He insisted that the method of preparing the book with notes on its coming 'action' was all wrong; atmospheric detail was the way. The writer must calculate the quantity of light, sound, colour and velocity there was to be in each chapter — literally on each page. When I asked him what measure I was to use in collecting my quantities of light, colour and sound — whether in pounds, feet or poods — he couldn't answer me. He drew a diagram; it looked like a page of book-keeping to me. We would have a long wrangle over it and once again he would murmur: 'Don't take any notice. I'm a bit wonky these days.' But on the very next occasion we met he would revive the whole thing. . . .

I am surprised I didn't get more suspicious. I ought to have known that he was not the person to get abject and apologetic about views which he felt strongly. The rigmarole, however, continued: he would condemn my work, then apologise and explain away his condemnation on the grounds of 'wonkiness'; then I would do my share by counter-apologising his apology and explaining for the umpteenth time that I was always open to criticism. But as if nothing had happened he was off again the next moment on the same crazy roundabout of condemnation, apology and explanation and I was hurrying to catch up with him. In the light of things one may well question which of us was the crazier.

I came away from him unnerved and harassed, as if from an altercation. He had put me in a most confused state of mind. In turn I both cursed him for tiring me out with futile arguments and experienced remorse at my own harsh response. I was almost glad when he didn't turn up at the library next day.

When he failed to turn up the day after that and the two days following I grew worried. I realised I must have hurt him. Then I was angry for his taking it so badly. 'He'll turn up when he gets over it,' I thought and tried to concentrate on my writing. But my remorse gradually submerged my anger.

I came along the next week and sat there all the time, looking up every time the doors opened. My attempts at doing anything were a pretence. I was extremely harassed.

On the first Monday of the new week I arrived with diminishing hopes, but with rather more determination to act in the event of his absence. I didn't quite know how. It would have to be a call at his lodgings late at night, I supposed. Nobody knew where to find him during the day. As I sat there fitful and restless, feeling it would now be an ordeal to wait until night to act, his 'friend' Sam walked through the swing doors. I quickly switched my eyes down to my work. I hoped he would think me busy and not come over.

I was all on the alert for his approach. At the end of three minutes I furtively raised my eyes again. He was studying a map on the wall across the room. 'Perhaps they're both arranging a tramp through England,' I thought, but without any real conviction. 'Perhaps he knows where Wise is!' I suddenly thought with rather more conviction. It was a desperate hope. I was now so worried that I was capable of asking his whereabouts from a stranger.

I stepped over and confronted Sam.

'Seen Wise lately?'

He gaped at me. I was already sorry I had got into conversation with him.

'No?' I said.

He continued to stare at me.

I raised my eyebrows questioningly.

He spoke with difficulty. 'He's dead,' he said. 'Dead!'

The rest of the day was spent in trying to piece together the story from the confused accounts given me by Sam and his mother. It was his mother who knew most. Wise had suddenly called at the house late one night, about a week back. He was informed that Sam was out and was asked to come in and wait. He shook his head without saying a word and turned away, crossing the road to take up a position under a lamp-post. Added to this strange behaviour he was without his coat, in spite of its being cold.

Sam stayed with a friend overnight. His mother beckoned to Wise once or twice from her window before going to bed. He remained unresponsive at the lamp-post. To her surprise he was still there in the morning.

This time he came into the house at her bidding. She made him lie down on the sofa. She was very upset by his appearance. He lay white, silent and staring. She hurried round to his home, but only the father was about and told her that his son 'could die like a dog for all he cared!'

She returned to find Wise gone. It was only three days later that she learned details of the sequel: he appeared to have run out wildly into the street in her absence and had been eventually picked up by the police and taken to the

Colney Hatch Asylum. Nobody was allowed to visit him there from the beginning until the end of his stay.

My inquiries to the Asylum for more information about the circumstances of his end and my request for an interview elicited this reply:

Dear Sir,

I have your letter of the 20th April. Mr. Ephraim Wise was admitted to this hospital in a state of acute Delirious Mania on 4th March 19—. In spite of treatment his delirium continued and he died of exhaustion on the 10th March 19—. He was not able to give any information with regard to himself and I am not in a position to give any opinion with regard to the circumstances which led up to his illness and admission to this hospital. Consequently there would be little to gain by such an appointment as you ask for.

Yours faithfully,

MEDICAL SUPERINTENDENT.

PART FOUR

*

CHAPTER 24

A Room of One's Own

My life was like a gipsy's during the next months. There was a different roof over my head almost every other week. All of them were East End roofs. I had been brought back to the district by a job. My efforts to get into a City factory had failed; I believe it is easier to get into the House of Lords without a title. Every one in a City clothing factory is a relative of every one else and spry indeed must be the stranger who wants to gate-crash this brotherhood.

And so much sooner than I had expected I was back in the East End with what I am forced to call my memories. The task of obtaining lodgings helped to push them into the background for a while. It was a task that claimed my whole attention. Bargaining over the rent was the least difficult part of the proceedings; it was the questionings and suspicions that were my real problem. These respectable Jewish folk couldn't quite accept the phenomenon of a Jewish youth living on his own. It didn't help much explaining that I was an orphan. They seemed to feel that no Jewish parents would do a thing so low as die and leave a young son all on his own. Had I looked the 'low-life' type it would have carried its own explanation; for outcasts from home are not at all uncommon. But here nature was against me. To fit the popular conception of the 'low-life' you must have a dark, vicious jowl, a precocious too-big-for-your-boots manner and a natty taste in hosiery. I believe, with all due modesty, that I looked the very antithesis of these things and to top it all I went around in a tweed jacket and flannels in all weathers, and hatless. I could have chosen no better method, had I deliberately set out to do so, of creating suspicion in Jewish hearts.

The first place I took a fancy to — or perhaps it would be more correct to say was not completely repelled by — was a three-roomed flat in a small block of tenements. I found later that three women shared it, two of them around the thirty-five mark and the third at least twenty years older. It was the third one who ran the show, but I never succeeded in discovering whether the younger two were her daughters or sisters. My own theory is that they were two daughters of hers who had been left by their husbands — for they exhibited a certain kind of anti-male prejudice that is the prerogative not of spinsters but of deserted wives. In fact as spinsters I am sure they would have doted on me. I do not state this as a flattery of myself, but as a characteristic of spinsters. Their unreasonable and intense dislike of me, however, seemed quite plainly the dislike of women who hold the unshakable belief that All Men Are Cads.

I had timed my call for late on a Sunday morning and my knock was answered by both. It was the first time I had seen two sisters so unlike each other physically. One was dark and bony, the other fair and solid. Both, however, were distantly hostile, as if I had called for alms, and their manner underwent no change even when I stated my purpose. All they did was to open the door a little wider for me to pass through. I found myself in a kind of miniature vestibule. The solid woman indicated a doorway on the left; I was surprised to discover, by another glance at her in passing, that her looks would have been quite pleasant had her mouth not been so thin and bitter.

Both remained behind me in the doorway. There was no effort on their part to practise salesmanship. Evidently

I could take it or leave it. There was, however, a kind of determinedness in their stand in the doorway which told me that 'leaving it' would not increase my popularity. It was not salesmanship, admittedly. It was intimidation.

I was relieved to find the room not too disappointing. It was large and distempered, with a bed in one corner and a gas-ring in the other. There were also the usual shelves and a cupboard.

'How much?' I said.

'Seven and sixpence,' said the solid woman defiantly.

I pretended to ponder it. She obviously expected demurrings and if I kept her in some suspense she might become more friendly when I ultimately gave in.

'All right,' I said at length.

She nodded briefly. The other woman made no sign at all, beyond regarding me intently and distrustfully. I never actually succeeded in getting a word out of her all the time I lived there. I had the impression she had taken a vow never to speak to a male again after her husband's desertion.

They both turned from the doorway and I had no other course but to follow them. We entered a door on the right of the 'vestibule'. I could see it was their living-room. I thought at first that the final arrangements were to be clinched there, but noticed that they were leading me into the adjoining bedroom. I heard a querulous voice calling from that quarter. The solid woman called back in Yiddish: 'The room is taken.' I followed her, mystified.

The two women took up a stand inside the doorway and then the solid one invited me in. As soon as I entered I knew that the old woman in the bed facing me was not sleeping late, but was bed-ridden, for no room that had not been occupied day and night continuously could have had the smell that room had. If you can imagine for yourself the smell likely to haunt a room in which every conceivable human function is performed, then you have guessed accurately at the smell in that room. My own powers of description fall short at that. I was pretty well used to smells of all kinds and though the one in that room was a bit of an eye-opener even to me I managed to betray no sign of it — comforting myself with the thought that my own quarters were at a safe distance.

The old woman in the bed — actually she seemed far from senile yet, but disarray adds years to a woman — regarded me with the same suspicion I had marked in the other two. You might have thought I was a delinquent who had been caught throwing stones at her window. There was a silence while she surveyed me through glistening spectacles. Her two daughters (or sisters) stood blocking up the doorway, as if determined that neither I nor the smell should escape.

Then the old woman spoke.

'You want the room, yes?' She seemed to have given great deliberation to the framing of that question.

I nodded and she exchanged a glance with the other two, as if I had incriminated myself in some way.

My patience had been slowly departing and the smell was making me really desperate.

'Look here,' I said. 'I thought you had a room to let. Well, is it to let or not?'

My peremptoriness was wasted, for she didn't get the complete English of that sentence and the solid daughter (or sister) had to translate it for her.

'Oh, sure, sure,' she said, when she had understood. 'But you understand, one must be careful with lodgers.'

'Have you got jewellery here?' I said sarcastically.

'Jewellery? You make fun of me, yes? If you knew my troubles! I had a lodger here once — he burnt up ten shillings a week gas!'

'I only have a cup of tea in the mornings,' I said.

She scratched thoughtfully at her hair.

'Mister,' she said suddenly, 'you've got no children, no?'

'No.'

'I had a lodger here once, he said he was single, and the day after moving in he brought a wife and children to live with him. Did you ever hear of such troubles for an old woman?'

'Missus,' I said, breathing deeply of the smell, 'I've got no children and I want a room. Do I get it or not?'

'Yes, yes, of course. But look, my son, in a friendly way where are your parents?'

'Dead.'

'Oy, Oy. So young, *mein Gott*! What is your age?'

'Nineteen.'

She swayed her head mournfully. I felt guilty and ashamed. The two in the doorway looked grimly sceptical. I ignored them.

'Do I get the room or don't I?' I said to the old woman.

'P'raps he'd better come back to-night?' called out the solid one in a kind of significant tone. She was obviously thinking of looking up my police record.

'I'm not coming back later or any other time!' I cut in before the old woman could reply. 'I've spent enough time here. I'm getting a room to-day and if you don't give it to me now I'm going to look for another one!'

I could see that some of my words had once again been lost on her, but this time she got the general drift of my outburst. She waved a weary hand at me.

'Give him, give him,' she moaned to the others. 'The room's been empty long enough. Let's not have more trouble. What will be, will be!'

'Well —— ' I was on the verge of remonstrating angrily, but the smell brought me up sharp and I realised that never before had there been a situation in which discretion was truly the better part of valour.

'I'll go and bring my bags,' I said to the old woman. 'Here's a deposit on the rent.'

'Yes, yes,' she moaned. 'What will be, will be!'

'Very true,' I said. The two in the doorway gave me

just enough room to pass.

Outside in the street I put my ear to the window for a moment in passing. That was how I discovered that neither of the two daughters (or sisters) was dumb or taciturn by nature. . . .

CHAPTER 25

No Place like Home

I⊤ was my own mistake to imagine that in surmounting
the initial difficulties of getting a room I had surmounted
them all. I began to feel a certain sympathy for those previous
tenants who had burned up ten shillingsworth a week of the
old woman's gas. This measure must have been necessitated
by their having to lock themselves in to escape her attentions.
No other alternative that I could see offered itself.

In the first place I had no key; the only one in existence
was in the possession of the old woman and she kept it
under her pillow. On what grounds she feared robbery or
rape, or whatever it was she feared, I could never get from
her. 'It's not right for strangers to have keys,' was all she
would tell me and I had no means of knowing whether she
was quoting the law, the Ten Commandments, the Five
Books of Moses, or some personal instructions from the
One Above. Unfortunately I only learned this news after
moving in with my bags. Perhaps I should have been prepared for that singular habit landladies have of mentioning
the disadvantages of their ménage only after you have paid
your first week's rent.

My keyless condition naturally brought me into more
frequent contact with the two daughters (or sisters) than
would otherwise have been necessary. It was they who
opened the door whenever I knocked. Actually the solid
one performed the task single-handed. As far as I could
gather the bony one would not touch doors in case it landed
her in conversation with a male caller. She was always there
in the background, though, a kind of shadowy presence. I

felt her eyes on me with each move I made.

Every evening without fail I was summoned to the bedroom to hear the old woman's 'complaints'. The first time it was on account of my late home-coming on the day I had moved in; the following day it was on the ground of using too much gas — the neighbours from the houses opposite in the courtyard apparently informed on me; the day after it was to defend the accusation of washing half-stripped before the window.

'Is that the right thing for a Jew to do?' said the old woman. 'I ask you!'

'Why don't you give me a curtain?' I retorted.

'A curtain? Look at him — he thinks I'm a millionaire, to give curtains away!'

'What do you expect me to do — wash in the dark, like a cat'?

'Cats,' the old woman moaned. 'Who's talking of cats? The troubles I bear! The other one burned me up ten shillings a week gas and this one shames me before the neighbours!'

I shrugged. 'I don't mind using the scullery for washing, if you'll let me.'

There was a grunt from the solid daughter (or sister) in the doorway. 'And p'raps you'd like to use the bedroom for sleeping in?' she called out.

'Not this one!' I said pointedly.

The old woman interrupted our cross-talk. 'Give him,' she moaned. 'Give him. Give him the scullery!'

They 'gave' me the scullery.

That was my first concession and like the concessions that followed it had all the nasty implications of a boomerang. For in 'having' the scullery I also had some extra attentions from the two women, whose business it was to see I didn't 'misuse' it. In pursuance of this duty they hovered around the scullery whenever I entered it and rushed in ostenta-tiously to 'clean it up' when I left.

The same kind of thing happened when I finally extracted a key from the old woman by the simple expedient of coming home late night after night and compelling her two daughters (or sisters) to get out of bed for me. But giving me a key didn't solve their worry. Whenever I let myself in I heard their door open and caught a glimpse of a disgruntled face and a sinister one through the crack. And at the closing of my bedroom door there would be a quarter of an hour's flurried reconnoitring of the bolts.

Every new 'concession' meant a new source of complaint. And every new complaint meant a new summons to the old woman's bedroom. That was my reason for giving notice at the end of a month. Mere complaints I could have borne — after nineteen years of practically nothing else. But that bedroom smell I could not. To leave home in order to come to that was in truth exchanging the frying-pan for the furnace.

Perhaps I would not have given up these lodgings so easily had I known the alternatives awaiting me in others. In not one was humiliation on a considerable scale spared me. It is surprising the variety there can be in what is in essence a simple history of dirt and discomfort.

In each new inspection of lodgings I kept a wary eye open for the vagaries of my previous ones. What I wasn't prepared for was the diabolical ingenuity of landlords. Each seemed to have his own individual brand of unpleasantness and an experience with one didn't necessarily equip you to deal with the next.

I therefore considered myself unusually lucky when I landed up in a place that was owned by a landlord who did not reside on the premises. This seemed to me, as it has no doubt seemed to innocents before and since, the Perfect Arrangement. People tend to forget that a landlord can make himself as unpleasant as he wishes without setting a foot on the premises. In fact, it is much more to his advantage to live *off* them, for it renders him inaccessible to complaints. An agent can perform all the dirty work necessary — and makes in addition a very suitable stalking-horse, for his duties begin and end with taking the rent and complaining to him is about as effective as complaining to the man next door.

This was the kind of lodgings I finally settled into. It seemed on the first day as good as anything I should be likely to get. It wasn't a particularly clean house, but dirt by then seemed to me as inevitable a part of life as London's smoky sky and it was no use brooding unnecessarily over what I thought to be one of the unalterable facts of existence.

Returning home on the second day I found a workman in my room fixing an electric meter to the wall. 'I thought electric light's included here!' I said to him.

'No use tellin' me,' he said laconically — and I could see he had used the retort to countless tenants before — 'Guv'nor's orders.'

The shock almost robbed me of my initial indignation at finding that the landlord had his own key to my room and I could do no more than demur feebly at this impropriety.

'Guv'nor says he gotta be able to get into tenants' rooms,' explained the workman. 'S'posin', now, f'r instance, you was to commit suicide?'

'It's very likely,' I said bitterly.

My life in the house from then on was an education in the art of slow torture. Each day a new atrocity revealed itself or was perpetrated at the behest of the 'Guv'nor'. The crowning point was reached in my discovery of a Smell. I don't mean the ordinary kind of smell that is part of the very architecture of a slum house. I had forgotten to notice that long ago. This new one was special, like the one in the old woman's bedroom. I encountered it when it was too late to do anything about it — in the slack season, that is — when moving was a financial venture quite beyond my means. The reason for the belatedness of this discovery was that the Smell pervaded the house only during the middle of the day and as the landlord had not mentioned it in his advertisement it was left for me to make the discovery during my unemployment.

By judicious investigation I traced it to the activities of the ground-floor tenant. Peering down from my landing two floors above I saw him come out of his room every day at twelve a.m., dishevelled and unwashed, and carry a bulky, covered dish to the ancient stove that stood in a nook by the lavatory. I heard the flare of the gas as he lit it. As soon as he lit it the Smell started and endured until he returned an hour later, still dishevelled and unwashed, to reclaim the dish and carry it back to his room, where, presumably, he ate it.

On each occasion I thought it was the last I had seen of him — that the whole thing was, in fact, a rather elaborate method on his part of committing suicide. But unfailingly, the day after, at the same hour and practically the same minute I was brought up sharp by the Smell seeping into my room and when I crept to the banisters after an hour's tense endurance it would be in time to see him emerge from his room and carry back the evil package with tenderly careful fingers, as if it were a dish of rare Eastern spices.

These are only a few sidelights of a life in lodgings and I feel justified in giving them the space I do for the reason that they formed an important part of the background to what were perhaps my most formative years and that whatever character I emerged with after these years cannot be understood except in relation to this as well as other aspects of my background.

The chief advantage for me was in helping me to get clear about my attitude towards home: for the first impulse to go into lodgings came from a revulsion from my former family life. Lodgings, though disillusioning, did not by any means bring repentance: a tyranny is no less a tyranny because there are other tyrannies as bad. And if a home life is tyrannical in its abnegation of individual independence, the 'independence' of a life in lodgings does not, on the other hand, compensate for its cold, inhuman atmosphere. Both alternatives are an outrage on human dignity and in my own case accentuated rather than solved the deadlock in my personal affairs.

CHAPTER 26

In Search of the Muse

It was at these lodgings that I began to take up again the writing I had stopped at Wise's death. The urge to say something was far stronger in me than the mere urge to use a pen, or I feel I should otherwise have been writing continuously for years before; for the fact is I had never felt awkward with a pen in my hand from my earliest days — yet while excelling at composition at school and being one of my club's 'star' contributors on the occasions I let myself be coerced into writing something for them, I had never felt the urge as a vital and pressing one until I went into lodgings. I don't mean that going into lodgings is a device for cultivating the urge to write. For even then I already knew in a vague way that going into lodgings was for me the logical 'next step' of my individual struggle and that with the step a certain something in me had reached maturity. This maturity, I believe, was some sort of realisation of where I stood in relation to the world. And accompanying this realisation also came the realisation of what I wanted to do with my life.

That what I wanted to do was not the most practical of issues worried me little. When you have found a reason for living its value in terms of cash is a secondary matter in relation to its value in terms of happiness. I don't think I had any illusions about my ambition to 'put down the East End on paper', as I called it. I knew it came out of a sheer physical necessity and when something is a sheer physical necessity you very rarely stop to ask questions.

My ideas for the actual task were hazy. The plan I

favoured was a family story, for it seemed to me that around that central unit of working-class society could be given as comprehensive a picture of that society as was possible on one canvas. I know now that ambitions of that sort are commonplace urges that derive very often from a too emotional reading of *The Forsyte Saga* or Tolstoy's *War and Peace*. That I had not read either of the two books does not, I also know, redeem the commonplaceness of the urge, but it does perhaps indicate that it was a genuine urge and not a mere literary one.

The other details of the work had not yet come to me. I had a gnawing and uncomfortable feeling that the task was too immense as yet for my immature years and outlook. That was what had kept me exclusively at short stories and sketches during my friendship with Wise. None were attempted with an eye to publication and looking them over now I bless the wisdom of this instinct, for the inevitable collection of rejection-slips resulting from a too premature desire to appear in print would have made a disheartening pile on my table.

I wrote these things quite plainly because I had to get something out of me or burst and though even to my own uncritical eye the result in each case was disappointing, the total effort was a great help in clarifying both my ideas about life and the problem of recreating it as literature.

While in work I could write only late at night and at week-ends. Actually I divided these 'spare time' periods into writing and reading. I felt it a desire as well as a duty to know what other people were saying about the modern world. Before wanting to write myself books had meant nothing to me: I had been trained by miseducation and upbringing to think of them as the prerogative of cranks and idlers and having about as little relation to life as the cultivation of fretwork. My own creative urge now awoke me to the feeling that I had missed something. The real trouble was in my not knowing where to start. Joining the library was a mere technical step forward; browsing among bookshelves does not necessarily improve your mind. Half the world's troubles in fact, one might say, come from an indiscriminate browsing among bookshelves and absorbing the poison of trivial or third-rate minds. What I wanted was the work of people who treated literature as a passion and not as a hobby or trade. This, to my perhaps undiscerning eyes, seemed to cut out at least seventy-five per cent of the current output and I didn't know where and how to find the other twenty-five per cent. Names on dust-jackets conveyed nothing to me. Nor did I care to ask the librarian for advice. I had a fear of making myself misunderstood. Asking for a 'good book' seemed to me an ambiguous request. A 'good book' is, after all, a personal interpretation. If you are partial to detective stories, then a 'good book' is a good detective story. I couldn't, on the other hand, bring myself to ask for a 'serious' or 'intelligent' book, for it sounded snobbish and highbrow — although 'serious' and 'intelligent' was the only way I can define my own particular wants in literature at the time.

As a start, therefore, I was compelled to spend my first period as a borrower in the non-fiction section. Here you were at least safe. There was no two-facedness about a book. When it called itself *A History of Man's Struggle with Nature* it was quite plainly and straightforwardly that — and not a handbook on tennis. Yet interesting and informative as such books were they were not quite what I was after. I was looking for what I now know is called creative literature. This could obviously only be found in the fiction department, but here the confusion brought deadlock. Something called *The Way of All Flesh* might be a profound study of human beings, but to judge it by its title alone it might equally be one of those unprofound studies of inhuman beings. One of the tasks of the censor in a civilised community would be, I think, to compel authors by law to use titles that correspond to the quality of their books.

In Search of the Muse

It was while I was doubtfully fingering the books on the non-fiction shelves one day that a voice spoke into my ear the words: 'You'll find the sporting section across the other side.' I looked up into the face of an old club-fellow.

'Oh, hallo,' I said, and finished off lamely there, for I didn't remember his name, although the rest of him was familiar. He hadn't altered since I had last seen him a year ago: a shabby, round-shouldered youth, with an air of being tolerant and friendly to life. He had had a studious reputation at the club, being an evening classes boy, so we hadn't mixed much. I was in the 'tough' set: that was his reason now for facetiously directing me to the 'sporting section'. 'Toughs' who read books are uncommon. I happened, however, to be an uncommon 'tough'; that is, a self-trained one. A childhood made miserable by bullying had determined me to reverse the balance in my youth, and this I had done, becoming, during my membership of the club, a very useful boxer by amateur standards, winning between the ages of fifteen and eighteen three Working Boys' Clubs championship cups at my weight and being chosen, together with another boy, to stage a three-minute exhibition before the Prince of Wales during his tour of the East End in 1928.

That had been over, long ago. Having to some extent redeemed the humiliations of childhood and in addition got some suppleness into my limbs I no longer felt cup-hunting ambitions. Only a case of mentally arrested manhood, I feel, can devote its entire energies to the delights of a gymnasium. So that I was slightly aggrieved at my former club-fellow's facetiousness and retorted: 'Why *sporting*? D'ye think I can't read?'

'I'm sure you can. Only wondered why you want to?'

'As a matter of fact,' I said with a pseudo-mysterious air, 'you're the only person I would confess it to — I'm looking for a *serious* novel. Can you help me?'

He regarded me searchingly through perpetually half-closed lids that looked as though he was straining to see without glasses and then he apparently decided to believe me.

'Come along, I'll show you where,' he said.

I joined him readily. 'What makes you ask *me*?' he said as we wound our way among the shelves.

'It was you that asked me,' I pointed out. 'But seriously, you've always looked to me as though you knew everything.'

'I know a bit about books,' he admitted.

'Wish *I* did.'

'Why?'

'Well — I'd like to read what great minds think of our crazy world.'

'They think it's crazy,' he said. 'Quite simple.'

'I prefer to see it in their own writing,' I grinned.

We had reached the fiction shelves and he began pointing out to me Who was Who. 'Your fancies may not be mine,' he said, 'so don't take this as the last word.'

'I never intended to,' I said.

He grinned at me kindly through those hazy, half-closed eyes of his. I could see he was too essentially modest to be hurt by any one's opinion of his shortcomings.

'I'm a good guide, anyway, you'll find,' he said. 'But what you want to do is read the current periodicals and get to know what's being written and published.'

'I don't know that I can afford them,' I said warily.

'Nor can I. You'll find the more important of them upstairs in the Reading Room.' He mentioned several by name.

'I'll try to get through them on Friday evenings after work,' I promised. 'You've been very helpful to me.'

'Let's meet here on Fridays,' he suggested. 'There's nobody I can talk books to. I'd much prefer to do that and a little less reading.'

I grinned. 'It sounds dangerous,' I said. 'But I'm sure it'll do me good.'

We parted soon after.

CHAPTER 27

Castles in the Air

DANIEL (for that was his name) and I were soon meeting much more frequently than on Fridays. I recognised in him a fellow 'misfit' — with the difference that he hadn't an aim in life, as I had. Nevertheless, he was by far the more contented of the two of us.

At the club I had known him for a hard-working youth. Now he informed me he had been unemployed a year. He had also stopped attending evening classes: with the introduction of mass-production methods in his wood-carving factory he had lost not only his job but all further interest in it. He could better afford this cynical gesture than most, for he was the only child of a small shop-keeper. His parents were less anxious about his unemployment than about his future. They were afraid he would forget what he had learned; his own worry was that he would 'never forget it as long as he lived' — the memory of the disappointment was so painful.

'Shouldn't think it's any use your waiting for modern production to return to the basis of the hand-loom,' I told him more than once. 'God knows when that'll happen.'

'I've got patience,' he grinned.

We met mostly at the library, for I had begun looking in on it in the evenings and it seemed that he spent the better part of the day there. He was an incorrigible 'browser'. He seemed to know a bit about every subject that came up in discussion.

'It's a wonder you don't try to put your knowledge to

use,' I said to him. 'Maybe you could be an instructor of a sort.'

He grinned good-humouredly.

'*You* might have illusions about me,' he said. '*I* haven't. There's no talent in what I do. You could also do the same if you hung around this place day and night. I'm a parrot that knows a few phrases, that's all.'

'I should have thought that description covers most teachers,' I said.

'Maybe. But to qualify for the parrot's job they have to pass certain tests and examinations. I've missed them. I'm a foundling parrot. I haven't got the official stamp that gets you into the fold.'

'Would you have liked it?' I said.

He pondered. 'Not now, I think,' he said. 'The disappointment of wasting six years in hard work and study seems to have killed all initiative in me.'

'Cynical words for twenty,' I said.

'True. One day I'll have to face things, I know.'

'That's just what I'm afraid of for you. Wouldn't the wisest thing be in the long run to knuckle down *now* to the idea that one has to work for a living and not for pleasure?'

'It would be the wisest thing,' he admitted. 'But it isn't the most tempting — and I'm an absolute slave to temptation.'

I remember thinking it strange at the time how most of our discussions turned ultimately upon our respective futures. It was of course largely my own doing. At nineteen I had an anxiety neurosis that most men don't get until they have a wife and children to support.

Being together late at night so often made it inevitable for me to invite Daniel into my room to continue one of our interminable discussions. I had held back as long as I could on account of my lodgings. I thought it would depress him, as it did me. But he accepted it with that same calm, contemplative interest that he accepted most things. I think it was merely to his encyclopedic mind A New Fact.

There was sufficient at that time in the house to shock anybody. Repeated requests to the landlord through his agent had failed to bring any improvement to the broken-down front door, so that night after night prostitutes were able to use the ground-floor passage for their rendezvous with clients. They had it completely to themselves in the absence of the dish-carrying tenant, who was presumably a baker. I had to pretend not to hear the dark scufflings on my way in every night, although in my innocence I committed, the first time I encountered it, the indiscretion of stopping to shoo loudly at non-existent cats. . . .

More discomforting were the activities of a prostitute who lived on the first floor — the one below mine. She did everything to advertise her calling except put out a red light at the door. Men came casually into the place at all times and though at first I took them for tenants, I soon realised that it would have needed a large-sized tenement to accommodate all the different faces I saw.

I think Daniel took these things much more in his stride than I. For a person of his limited experience he seemed to have a remarkable capacity for understanding the unusual.

'This is the place to write about,' he said — we had already discussed my writing often before — as we sipped tea before the half-ruined gas-fire in my room. He followed the remark with a kind of smacking of the lips, in the way of a journalist encountering 'a scoop'.

'That's not quite what I'm after,' I replied.

'No? Then what?'

'I don't really know. I only know clearly what I'm not after: I'm not after compiling a kind of Borough Council report on the housing conditions in Stepney — although incidentally that's a job that ought to be done. I hope some public-spirited Borough Councillor will do it one day.'

'And *your* job?'

'I don't know. Of one thing I feel certain, though: it's got to come *not* from an impressive collection of statistics lying beside me on the table, but from a kind of passion — the sort of thing, you know, that carries an ambitious swimmer across dangerous rapids he hasn't previously navigated. I believe,' I said, 'that's about as clearly as I can put my idea into words.'

'It sounds tremendous,' Daniel said thoughtfully. 'But it also sounds like something impossible.' He grinned. 'Swimming rapids always does! Somebody manages it now and then, though. That must be your inspiration. '

Unemployment caught me shortly and Daniel and I met often during the day. On several occasions he actually accompanied me on job-hunting expeditions and I suspect that he breathed with relief each time I walked out of a building into which I had ventured to apply for work — for in the periods that I could forget the looming shadow of the Means Test we spent some entertaining hours building our air-castles. Strictly speaking they were *my* air-castles, but he joined most enthusiastically in their construction. Chief and air-castle Number One was the Great Book on the East End I intended to write. If I had a few *little* doubts Daniel had none at all. He was obviously the faithful rather than the discerning friend.

I questioned him about it once — not because I wanted flattery, but because I wanted to share his conviction if I could.

'You worry a lot,' he said. 'That's why. Or to put it artistically — you suffer.'

'You mean I'm a grumbler?'

'A *sufferer*. It's different. A grumbler suffers for himself only. A sufferer suffers for everybody. To be a sufferer you must have the imaginative gift.'

'You ought to be able to do the job much better than I with all that understanding,' I said.

'Not at all; it's an understanding from outside. Feeling is the important thing. Or *imaginative* understanding, if you want to call it that.'

'And what makes you think I have this?'

'Because in your talk you dramatise suffering. It's not an isolated incident in the day, as to most people, but part of a pattern — the pattern of the world we live in. Whatever you see has for you symbolic meaning. You see more than his dawdling gait, for instance, in that man there across the road: perhaps a reluctance to return to an unpleasant wife, or a nasty job — ideas which in turn suggest a host of other details that go to make up a story. Probably in your eyes *I'm* a sufferer.' He grinned: 'The symbol of a wasted life! I think you feel all these things partly because you suffer for yourself and have a knack of identifying others' suffering with your own. You're a peculiar blend of self-pity and the Christian spirit.'

'If I am, I don't seem to be any different from you — if I'm to judge by the fact that you understand what I feel.'

'That's not true. I may understand what you feel, but I don't feel what you feel. When *I* see a man with holes at the back of his socks, to me he's a slut. When *you* see a man with holes at the back of his socks you see a background with it: lodgings, loneliness, defeat — a host of things that personally I can't visualise or be bothered to get absorbed into.'

'All I can say to that,' I said, 'is, that though you say you can't write my book, it's pretty obvious that you'll be able to knock it to pieces if it doesn't turn out right.'

'I think I agree with you there,' grinned Daniel.

CHAPTER 28

Birth Pains

IT is strange that at the time the continuance of unemployment did not dampen my urge to write, but sharpened it — a condition I have never experienced since. Real stark hunger was something new for me and while a part of me hated it another part revelled in it, for it distorted me in my own eyes as the symbol of something profoundly sorrowful.

One night when sleep became difficult for the hunger gnawing my stomach and the strange tumult in my head I dressed and went out into the cold, grey streets of East London's dockside. I saw wretches huddled in doorways and ragged prostitutes slinking by walls and I wept at their misery and my own. There arose in me at the same time the desire to scream the story of our common fate into the face of the world. It soon took me like a fever and I tramped towards home with my hunger forgotten in the ecstasy of a new-found resolution.

I sat at my table and wrote without pause. I wrote what I had seen. It was not a story — it was a statement. Tears once again flowed down my face as I re-lived the experience on paper, but they must have been tears engendered by the monstrous forms taken by self-pity, for when I re-read what I had written next day I was unable to recapture my original emotion. I saw the scene in something of its sordidness, but not its tragedy. The tragedy, it seemed, had only been in my heart.

From that moment on my ideas found their greatest stimulant in Night. Night became for me what sunshine is for the poet. I have also learned since then to distrust the word written at night, although often respecting the emotions that inspire it. It was otherwise then; and I was made miserable by the futility involved in continually producing masterpieces at night that showed up as counterfeits in the morning. Of this incoherent activity I did not tell Daniel a word. We discussed mostly not my writing but the books we read. I had had a sudden reversion from the moderns to the Masters, finding more in every way of what I wanted in Dostoievsky and Balzac than in any except the most outstanding contemporaries. I have always since favoured rather those writers who get into a passion about life than those who lay it bare before you like a dissected corpse and this to-day has left me better acquainted with the work of French and Russian writers than with English ones — whom I have rarely been able to read as enthusiastically with the exception of what I would term the satirists, starting with Defoe and continuing along the line to his present-day descendants. I have a feeling that it was these two opposite influences that contributed partly to my own inchoateness, for passion and satire are, stylistically speaking, at opposite ends of the pole, although in origin and motive they may be identical. I mixed them merely according to mood or caprice. You can imagine the effect of religiously lyrical outbursts often coming in the middle of what were intended to be detached and blandly ironic discourses.

These confusions did not encourage confidence in my more ambitious plan of the Great Book. I still knew nothing beyond the fact that it was to be a 'family' story; except that in the depths of my heart I was convinced that this family story would not be 'just a family story' in the way that so many books are 'just a love story'. Yet why not? My intentions were still so much more hazy than my emotions. I could see the effect but not the method: it would be a book about both great things and small things; it would explain my own family and, in some significant though lesser way, all families; my own life, and all poor lives; East End Jews and all persecuted peoples; my own suffering world and the whole suffering world. This was the Great Book towards whose fashioning I looked forward with anxiety, but also with an eagerness that in those moments when it possessed me completely could send me untiringly through London's streets in forgetfulness of my hunger.

I believe it was the two main obsessions in me at the time that brought the idea of the book to fruition. One was the estrangement with my family, the other the memory of sorrowful faces seen in my nocturnal perambulations through the dockside. The picture repeatedly came to me of the world as a vast family in decay. My task would be to write its history in miniature. It would be the history of a poor Jewish family, but in some of its deeper implications it would also be a sort of history of the human family. An idea for its opening scene started me off along the entire train of thought: I saw a boy being taken prematurely out of school by his parents. Probably the memory of my own personal experience in that field is one from which I subconsciously date the starting point of the conflict with my own parents. For it struck me as a stimulating opening: at one and the same time it launched a story, a psychological conflict, an opportunity for character-building, and supplied the setting of a particular environment. From then on the onus rested on me to give positive form to this outline and etch in its delicate shades.

The story, when I began it, proved much harder going than I had imagined. Details could not struggle up to the surface of my mind for the fevered emotions that stifled them. The 'visions' that came to me were the few high peaks of the story and it was these that kept my eagerness at a pitch rather than the daily efforts. I could see the decay of the family far more clearly than I could the development that preceded it, but while its details intrigued me I was worried by the necessity of having to write the substance of a story before I could bring in its dénouement. All the high peaks in this process of decay were tragic ones and I think it was that which made them clearer for me than the rest of the book, for they were each and every one of them a particular form taken by my self-pity and in revelling in them to the exclusion of all else I could in that way revel interminably in my own plight.

Between my periods of nocturnal creativeness I endured bleak periods of sterility. They were all the bleaker because of the other interludes. I existed between the poles of a feverish contentment and a low-spiritedness during which I remembered my hunger and every forgotten pain.

I probably suffered in keeping my work a secret from Daniel. I could not bear to risk discouragement in so early a stage of its progress. He must have attributed these moods of mine to hunger, for following the worst ones he invariably brought a present of food. These were mostly sandwiches and their crude and hurried packing hinted at domestic worries. The suspicion was strengthened when I noticed that he was gradually giving up lengthy dinner-times — returning to me after having what must have literally amounted to 'a bite'. A little later he informed me he was keeping his eyes open for odd jobs in people's houses in order to 'keep his hand in'.

One evening he turned up to my room in an unusually flustered state, as if he had been walking hard (or working hard — but I dismissed that possibility) and wheezed in a perspiring good humour: 'May have a little job for you. Nothing tremendous — but I think there's food in it.'

'Yes?'

'It's in a home for vagrant boys or something,' he said. 'I'm making them a few cupboards — a blasted busybody of a neighbour told my Ma they were looking for a cheap handyman!' He grinned. 'Can't refuse a job that's stuck right under my nose, it'll look as if I don't want to work. . . . The fact is, they're paying me practically nothing — you know what these charity places are: they expect you to *give*, not take from them. I'll get meals free there, though, and that's chiefly what I took it for.'

'You don't need meals.'

'But you do! Here's my plan. They're not only short of a handyman, they're short of most things. One of them's an instructor.'

'An instructor?'

'A *physical training* instructor. The boys have got the loan of a gymnasium, but nobody to supervise them. I've told 'em I've got the very man. It'll give you the pretext for dropping in at the Home on occasion — meal-times, if you've got any sense!'

'I'm grateful,' I said, bewildered. 'But I'm hardly in the mood for physical training just now.'

'You won't be in the mood for anything at all if you don't eat!'

I was silent and he added briskly, 'You'll turn up at about seven o'clock next Tuesday. It's their boxing night. They go off to the gym right after supper — and supper is at seven. D'ye catch on?'

'Boxing after a meal?' I said, horrified.

'You've got to adapt your boxing to your meals now,' said Daniel, 'not your meals to your boxing, like in the old days.'

'It'll be an experience, anyway,' I said gloomily.

'That's the way to view it. It'll keep you alive for the Great Book.' He grinned. 'Dead men, you know, tell no tales!'

CHAPTER 29

The Lord is My Shepherd

In spite of Daniel's sanguine hopes it did not prove practical to visit the Home on any other occasions than official ones, for the Warden had a sharp eye for idling and would have soon seen through my little game. Consequently my net profit out of the post of 'instructor' amounted to no more than a couple of free meals a week — taken on the two evenings that the boys were lent the use of a gym belonging to a Toc H officers' unit stationed in the Tower of London Barracks.

Daniel confessed his own disappointment.

'Still, if the worst comes,' he consoled, 'you're sure of at least two meals a week.'

I didn't tell him how little I got out of even those two meals in the depressing atmosphere of the Home. The place reminded me of the workhouse in *Oliver Twist*. The inmates there couldn't have looked much different from these: mostly boys with the gaunt, tired faces of old men. A large number of them were North Country vagrants who had been picked up on the road near London or on benches by the Embankment. Here they stayed until work was found them — a fate often much worse than that from which they had sought refuge: for there was nothing they could do except serve on the staff of some overworked restaurant kitchen. In cases where the wages were too small for them to live in lodgings they remained on at the Home in exchange for three-quarters of their earnings.

For the rest of the inmates the Home was a prison, except that there were no cells. The wide world was their cell —

they were sent out into it every morning after tea and a slice of bread-and-margarine, with nothing to see them through the day until the evening meal at seven except a bread-and-jam sandwich.

At the close of the evening meal they were shepherded upstairs into the common-room. This was a small, bare place with two chairs, a table and three ancient periodicals, and in the absence of any real facilities for recreation it is hardly surprising that the evening often terminated in a 'rough house' — bringing prompt and stringent intervention from the Warden. Usually the penalty was loss of next morning's 'meal'. In the more flagrant cases expulsion followed; the Warden would promulgate it on the spot:

'Brother David, put on your jacket and get out! Don't come back to-night — or any more!'

Every one was 'brother' in this Christian paradise, the relationship resembling the one shared by Cain and Abel.

These were my 'pupils'. It can be imagined how much zest I had for the job, knowing as I did that the physical jerks I subjected them to was an insult to their hungry stomachs.

I came to detest myself for having any truck with the place at all. I disliked going there even on the two evenings that I was presumed to be profiting from it; when I returned to resume work on my book late at night I could not keep the thought of the place out of my head. Beside its fierce reality my 'family' story seemed a trivial distraction. I would sit inactive at my table, thinking interminably of scenes for which I had a feeling but no pen.

In the middle of all this a conflict with my landlord (or rather his agent) seemed imminent again: I had come to the conclusion that my gas supply was being tampered with. It was costing me more. I looked for tell-tale signs on the meter, but it conveyed nothing and I could think of no other explanation beyond the impossible one that the landlord came and cooked his meals in my absence.

The Lord is My Shepherd

I had waited a while, in order to make sure that my facts were not suspicions — but when on a Sunday evening the gas-fire began to die down a half-hour after I had put twopence in the slot I knew that my suspicions were, quite truly, facts. I asked Daniel, who was with me, whether he could smell an 'escape'.

He shook his head. 'But, of course,' he added, 'you've got to remember how expensive a gas-fire is.'

I was unimpressed.

'At the rate it's burning here', I said, 'you couldn't sell a gas-fire even in Mayfair. I don't believe that's the explanation.'

'I've got an idea,' Daniel said abruptly. He had been regarding the walls thoughtfully. He rose and beckoned me.

'Let the gas go out,' he suggested. 'We'll have a peep at your neighbour.'

'Didn't know I had one,' I said, mystified, as I followed him to the door.

He opened it quietly and put his ear to the adjacent door in the passage. 'When I give the sign with my hand,' he whispered, 'put a penny in the slot and light the gas.'

I stood watching him from the doorway. He had taken up a kneeling position, with his eye to the keyhole, but I couldn't tell what he was seeing, for his face gave me no sign. Then his hand went up slowly. I hurried back to carry out his instructions and returned again. I was in time to hear the distinct pop of the gas being lit in the next room. We exchanged a look. Daniel rose, dusted his trousers and re-entered my room.

'Carrying on the landlord's good work,' I said bitterly. 'I'm being attacked on two fronts.'

'Only one thing to do,' said Daniel thoughtfully. 'You of all people can't afford to hand out charity. You'd better go and knock at his door.'

I nodded, reluctant in spite of my anger, But when I knocked at the door I did so boldly, so as to give myself confidence in my cause.

'Come in,' said a voice that was so youthful that it was almost piping.

I opened the door, but remained in the doorway with Daniel. Two people turned round to face us from chairs at the gas-fire; they were a boy and girl, but I was less surprised at their youth than at their condition. They looked as though they had not washed, eaten, or slept for days. It showed mostly on the boy, whose gauntness would have been noticeable even among the vagrants at the Home. The girl was small and looked as though she would have been buxomly pretty in better circumstances. She turned away listlessly from us after a glance. Only the boy's thin smile was friendly and welcoming.

I had no notion of what to say. I was stunned by the look of the room — empty of all furniture save a small, wooden table and a kind of moth-eaten couch. Even the dirty floorboards were uncovered.

Daniel spoke for me. 'It's about the gas-fire,' he said quietly. 'We're from next door, you know.'

'Oh.' The youth had caught on and was suddenly shamefaced. The girl took no notice of us at all.

'I'm sorry, sir,' he said in a thin, humble voice to Daniel. There was a distinct North Country accent in his words. 'It was for my wife. I'll turn it down again, sir.'

'Your wife?'

'Yes, sir.'

'Wait a minute,' I cut in hastily as he bent to the gas-fire. He looked up in surprise.

'Is she ill?' I said.

'She's pregnant, sir. This is her only evening off. I don't mind for myself, sir, but it's hard for her in the cold.'

The girl looked up at us again at the words. Her eyes were round and defiant, like a schoolgirl's. I felt sick with misery.

'Why not come into the other room, both of you?' Daniel said briskly. 'Might as well share one room, seeing that we're sharing one fire!'

The girl became as humble as her husband when she saw that our intentions were friendly. Both answered readily to our questions as they munched the bread-and-cheese we had pressed upon them. Newcastle was their home town. They had married on the strength of their dreams of London and tramped here to find the fulfilment of them almost immediately after the marriage ceremony. Since then they had done almost everything to keep alive. They were at their last ditch: the boy was unemployed, and the girl was at work in the kitchen of the landlord's own house for which she received twelve shillings and sixpence a week — twelve shillings of which was returned to the landlord as rent for living in the room next door mine.

'Then you really work for sixpence a week?' I said.

'I suppose so, sir,' she said slowly.

'How do you both eat?'

'Mary fetches me bits from the kitchen sometimes,' cut in the husband, giving her a fond smile, 'and gets what she can for herself while she's there. It's the cold that's really the worst. Isn't it, lass?' he said, turning to her again.

She nodded dumbly.

'And I'm really sorry about that gas, sir,' he said to me.

'Never mind that. What are you going to do about your wife?'

'Ay,' he said gloomily. 'That's the real trouble. She's six months on the way, but landlord's wife won't give her no time to go to hospital.'

'What about the law?' I cried.

He gave me a surprised look. 'It ain't owed to Mary by law, sir,' he said. 'She's free to leave if she don't like things.'

'Free?' I said bitterly.

He looked at me in a humble silence, as if apologetic at causing me a problem.

CHAPTER 30

Success

THE problem of the young pair was for me a problem of the house again, like the Smell and the prostitutes — but much more urgently in need of a solution than either. Such misery was something it was truly impossible to live next door to in acquiescence.

I called them both in again next evening to discuss the position. The husband, it seemed, spent most of his time at the Exchange, in the hope of eventually worming some sort of maintenance out of the authorities. I felt it was less than no hope at all: for he had very few stamps on his card and God knows how grudgingly even those who are lawfully entitled to the dole get it given them!

It was Daniel who afterwards suggested having a try at getting Tom (the husband) some kind of daily nourishment at the Home to keep him going in his job-hunting efforts.

'They're not exactly shepherds to every stray sheep,' I said doubtfully.

'Perhaps not. But he's a very convincing case, you must remember. He's a walking advertisement of hardship, if ever there was one.'

'Well, I can only hope you succeed — for my peace of mind as well as for his. It's no joke living next door to such misery.'

I felt a great easing of the burden when Daniel got his way at the Home. It was agreed to provide Tom with a mid-day meal, daily. While this move did not change his position radically it did at least raise him to a level somewhere around my own — which, if not a great comfort to

him, was certainly one for me: I didn't have to feel so sorry
for some one who was enduring no more than I was myself,

There still remained the girl's dilemma. Daily we expected
a breakdown — although she and Tom made great play
about her 'toughness'. I had been for going straight to the
landlord, but Daniel warned against such a move:

'It might only have the effect of getting her the sack
and where'd they both be then?'

The only immediate hope we could see was in Tom —
for with a good solid meal in the daytime to fall back on
there seemed a larger likelihood of success for him in his
job-huntings.

I can only suppose that the relief at getting at least a
little something done after so long an acquiescence was
responsible for the new energy I suddenly found for my
book. It was also now a matter of the utmost urgency for
me to get out of this strange house of sorrow; it didn't
matter if I went to nothing better, as long as it was to
something different. Yet I could not make a move till I
had the book done: for I knew that if I didn't do it then
it would never be done; I had a constant fear of not finishing
it — a fear much greater than the fear of finishing it badly.
I felt that a dreadful future lay before me and a future into
which I was to be landed without having struck even one
frail blow for the past seemed to me a future not only dreadful but unthinkable.

The next fortnight was for me a confusion of nervously
sporadic, but satisfying, activity. I knew I was getting the
job done, even if it did not bear too close examination. And
my happiness at the final result was far greater than my
anxiety at its quality. When I looked at the bound manuscript before me the realisation that I had succeeded in
producing a kind of youthful testament gave me a joy that
no other reservations could intrude upon. Even the fact that
the manuscript was handwritten did not depress me: I was

sure that its fierce appeal must grip the publisher, like it did me, to the point of disdaining all other considerations.

It was only the thought of my secretiveness with Daniel that remained a worry; and I told myself that the desire to surprise him with the book's acceptance could be submitted to him later as a legitimate reason for my concealing its creation.

I sent it off to a publisher whose name I had often seen printed on the jackets of novels about unemployment.

The period that immediately followed this act was one that I can only describe as light-hearted. I felt myself on the brink of vague new hopes. I believe now that it was relief at getting a worrying job done that gave me the feeling — rather than any positive expectations.

Reaction came with slow and dogged certainty. I began in turn to feel restive, anxious and finally conscious once more of an appalling purposelessness in my life. Now there was not even the writing of the book to give me the illusion of being different to any ordinary uprooted person. In any case I had a growing conviction that I had not pulled off the job. The knowledge that I had rushed it through gradually assumed an all-dominant importance.

I now stayed in the house a lot, in a kind of paralysis of introspection and lethargy. I took a depraved pleasure in pondering the disappointing aspects of both my book and my home. Sometimes I thought I was mad and when I didn't think I was mad I was conscious of being profoundly and vastly unhappy. It was the better feeling of the two when I thought I was mad. It made me interesting to myself and kept me from the ever-present temptation to commit suicide.

I would sit and listen to every sound in the house. There seemed more sounds now than there had been a fortnight back — or perhaps I was more sensitive to them in the lack of a task to do. I thought a great deal about each sound — I played endlessly with its meaning and significance and these were always the best moments, for then I came nearest to thinking I was mad.

I got into the habit of starting up at footfalls on the floor below. Repeatedly I went to the door to see who had made them, although I knew they could only belong to persons who were so well known to me that I was sick of the sight of their faces.

I took to going out to the landing at noon, to anticipate the emergence of the dish-carrying tenant on the ground floor. I would wait almost tensely for his door to open and was conscious of a great relief when he came out bearing his evil burden. Somehow in this daily act of his I saw symbolised the eternal unchangeableness of Man and I was awed and uplifted, as if at an example of superior fortitude.

One morning he glanced up as he came out. He had never done this before. I was leaning over the banisters, quite unprepared. I couldn't withdraw without revealing that I had been standing there for the purpose of watching him, so I remained where I was, feeling guilty and rather stupid.

He stopped and called 'Hallo!' to me in a thick, blurred voice and smiled up. His smile was a false, ingratiating kind of smile and only made me feel more awkward in that I could see no reason for his wanting to ingratiate himself with me.

'Hallo,' I replied, rather lamely. I made a move to withdraw casually.

He remained where he was with the dish in his hand, calling up in what I can only describe as an affable leer, 'How's the young couple next door, old chap?'

I was too taken aback to make anything but an automatic reply. 'All right,' I said, secretly infuriated by his cheek and my own timidity.

'Thought you're not in much in the mornings?'

'No, not usually,' I muttered.

'Care for some dinner?' he said, indicating his dish.

'I'm not hungry,' I said hastily.

'Lucky feller. It's cheaper that way. Well, I must be getting along with my own.'

I nodded and this time withdrew, feeling confused and discomfited at his shoddy familiarity and the memory of his sly, glinting eyes.

I gave him a lot of uneasy thought in the next days, but as I didn't hear anything more and was myself careful to keep away from the landing, I dismissed him from my mind as an unpleasant busybody who had been hearing gossip about myself and the couple next door from the landlord's agent and was not discreet enough to keep it to himself.

It was Mary's return home with a bad headache one night that reminded us of a problem we had left unsolved. Tom had brought us in to look at her. She lay at full length on the couch with her coat on. We sat at the end of it. Tom hovered around restlessly.

'She says she don't feel too bad,' he kept repeating. 'But it makes you worried — her being in her condition.'

'I keep telling him he's wrong, sir,' Mary muttered through half-closed eyes. 'I've had headaches before.'

'We ought really to get you a doctor from somewhere, somehow,' said Daniel.

'Oh no, sir. It'll pass. My Ma had seven children and she's alive and well.'

I couldn't quite see what that proved, but neither I nor Daniel contradicted her.

'It's the worry more than anything else, sir,' she said slowly. She gave Tom a kind of sorrowful glance.

'Don't be silly, Mary!' he said impatiently.

'Tom's getting along all right for the moment,' I said. 'He eats at least as well as you.'

'I'm worried about him,' she repeated. 'He'll — he'll do something . . . then there'll be more trouble.'

'Mary!' Tom said.

She ignored him. 'I wish you'd stop him going around with the man downstairs,' she said in a low voice. 'He's a real bad 'un.'

Tom looked a mixture of sheepishness and anger.

'Didn't know you knew the chap, Tom,' I said mildly. 'I thought he slept most of the day.'

'So he does!' cut in Mary vehemently. 'It's in the nights they see each other. He kept Tom out with him until five the other morning!'

I exchanged an uncomfortable look with Tom.

'I thought the fellow was a baker,' I said.

'He's no baker! He's — he's — I'd rather not say, sir. He's no good for Tom, anyway. They bin scheming together and I know he'll get Tom into trouble. I know it!' She was very wrought-up and kept raising her head for each sentence and letting it fall back wearily at the close.

'Don't worry,' Daniel said. 'If it means all that to you I'm sure Tom'll stop going around with the man. Eh, Tom?'

Tom hesitated, pursed his lips and nodded slowly.

Mary looked relieved in a kind of doubtful way and I followed up hastily, saying, 'Now you'd better take it easy if you don't want to have to go to the hospital in the morning. We'll make you some tea while you get ready for bed.'

We shepherded Tom out between us as we left. He came uneasily into my room and sat down at the table while Daniel and I got busy with a kettle of water and some sandwiches.

There was a silence while we worked, until Tom caught my eye and blurted out: 'Well, what's a feller to do, sir, when things are so bad?'

'What's a feller been doing?' said Daniel, turning from the stove.

'Oh, nothing,' muttered Tom. 'Nothing dreadful, sir.'

'You will do, though, if you chum up with the bloke downstairs — from what I've heard of him.'

'He ain't bad,' said Tom sullenly. 'Anyway, he don't pay no rent!'

'What?' I said incredulously.

'No, he don't! And I believe him when he says so. He's got a hold over the landlord,' Tom added triumphantly. 'It takes a smart man to do that!'

'You mean blackmail?' I said.

'*I* ain't afraid of fancy names!'

Daniel burst out laughing. 'Who is? In my opinion it's good luck to anyone who can get one over on your landlord. But I don't think *you* will, Tom — that's all.'

'You think I'm a mug?' Tom said bitterly.

'No.·Blackmail's a losing game in the end, that's all. Your friend downstairs may be lucky for the moment, but he'll get into jail in the end — and he's trying to take you there with him.'

Tom was silent.

'You've gotta think of Mary and — and the child,' I stammered, feeling stupidly fatherly. 'She'd be lost if you got into trouble.'

He nodded and we dropped the subject. But I had a feeling he was slyly keeping his own counsel.

Daniel stayed the night with me, for in spite of our reassurances to Mary we had our premonitions and felt we ought to be on hand in case an ambulance was needed in the middle of the night or first thing in the morning.

We didn't fall asleep until late and I was startled when Daniel's tap on my shoulder awoke me after what seemed a two-minute doze. My first thought was the girl. Then I saw that Daniel was dressed.

'It's all right,' he grinned in response to my query. 'They're both getting up. Here's a letter for you that just came.'

I took it gingerly from him. It looked official, like most of my correspondence.

'The Exchange?' I suggested distastefully.

'Maybe the landlord.'

'That's no improvement!'

Then as a sudden light struck me I whispered, 'I believe
——' and couldn't say any more. I tore open the flap.

There was a thin package and when I opened it a single
paper fluttered loose: it was a letter from the publisher.
I was half-way through it before I looked up and said to
Daniel sheepishly: 'It's about my book. I finished it and
sent it off without showing it to you because I wanted to
give you a surprise.'

He stared at me incredulously and came over to the
bed to read the letter with me. It was as follows:

Dear Sir,

We now have a report on the MS. which you submitted
to us, and regret that we feel that we should not be justified
in publishing it in its present form. But at the suggestion
of our Reader we are sending you a copy of his report,
which will give you his opinion on the possibilities of your
book, with which we substantially agree. You probably
know that it is not usual to pass on a reader's report of a
novel to the author, but we feel that in this case it is the
best thing to do, and hope that if you feel that the report
is helpful to you, you will let us know to what extent you
are willing to fall in with its recommendations. Meanwhile,
we are retaining your MS., until we hear from you.

'Well!' said Daniel.

'Let's see the report,' I said huskily.

It filled three pages of close type and was headed by a
bracketed statement in which the reader informed the
publisher that he had allotted more than the usual time
for a reading of the book for the reasons that, 'a working-
class novel of East London is a rare and eventful thing',
and that 'the book is unusually long — some 130,000 words
(as long as two small novels) . . .'

There followed an outline of the story, concluding with the observation that 'the entire novel is an ambitious attempt to depict the life of a family as sons and daughters grow up. . . .'

Then came a section headed *Remarks* that was as lengthy as the outline:

'. . . the book is unnecessarily long. It needs ruthless pruning. It is sometimes almost unbearably tedious — I am aware that the life of working people is often dull and monotonous; but the working-class artist does not himself have to be dull in order to convey that. The test, in fact, of his art is that he convey monotony and routine and dullness *without* wearying the reader and thus defeating his own object.

'. . . The style is in places vigorous — in a few instances achieving a swift-passing, poetic beauty; this is particularly the case in his workshop descriptions. But, time after time, the vigour will fall into redundant, sentimental and rhetorical writing. . . .

'. . . Characterisation, I must repeat, is best in the casual characters. In fact, in this book, I fear the fatal weakness is that the garnishings are better served up than the joint. There are isolated episodes that the Editor of *New England* — whom I took the liberty of asking to glance at the book — wishes, with the author's permission, to publish very shortly in the above periodical. . . .'

The final section was titled *Conclusion*:

'While I fear there is no hope for the publication of the book in its present form, I would greatly regret it if the writer were to abandon attempts at writing in future, because of this. Despite the faults of the book, it is apparent that the author *can write* — he needs more practice, I should say, and, above all, *self-discipline*; not to be so easy on himself, not to let himself get away with one over-facile long paragraph after another; to study the superior effectiveness of economy of adjectives — of a lean, iron-ribbed strength in language and even, occasionally, the explosive force of *under*-statement. This book suffers greatly from *over*-statement. The story of this Jewish family *should* be published. The author knows his milieu and his people. He might, I suggest, start by drastically cutting down the present book — then 'vetting' the style of what is left. And then, in the light of his expanding knowledge of human character, infusing a touch of deeper penetration into his treatment of the family. He is perhaps a little too *near* them to be fair with them — a few more months may help.

'. . . Novels — or even attempts at novels — of this type are so rare, that the author should certainly be encouraged to continue writing. This first production is really remarkable in its sustained effort, showing that he has the drive to write.'

I lay back on the pillow at last, still clutching the report. Daniel gripped me by the arm.

'Well,' he grinned, 'you don't look very happy for a man that's had a success at last.'

'You mean the excerpts for *New England*?'

'Of course!'

'I can't pretend I'm not glad about that,' I said. 'But I don't think I'll appreciate it fully till later. At the moment I can only think of the main result — failure.'

'Depends on one's point of view.'

I shook my head. 'When a man sets out to swim a river but only gets to one of the small islands in the middle of it — it isn't even a minor success: it's a failure. And when I set out to produce *the* Great Book — and only produce another article, well, it's the same thing.'

'It's certainly a disappointment. But now you must look on the positive side. You've got a foothold in some kind of a future.'

I smiled, feeling very happy suddenly. 'Part of the money for those articles,' I said, 'can pay Tom and Mary's fares back to Newcastle. There's no future at all until I get them off our hands!'

'Let's go and tell 'em,' grinned Daniel. 'It'll buck 'em like anything to know they can get out of this!'

I sprang out of bed for my clothes.

I shall always remember it as the first morning that I was glad to open my door on the world.

Printed in Great Britain
by Amazon